NORTHUMBERLAND STRONGHOLDS

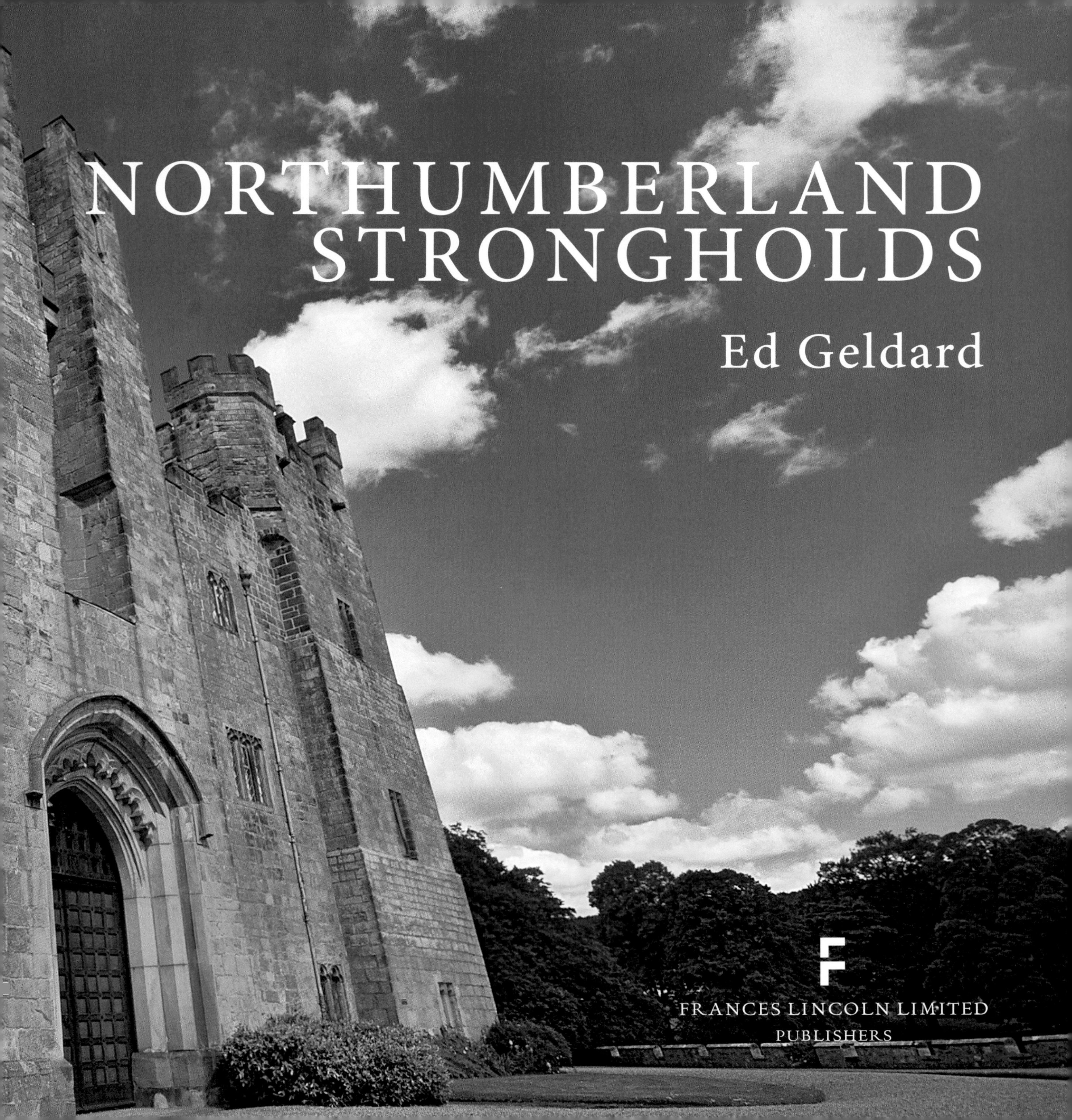

NORTHUMBERLAND STRONGHOLDS

Ed Geldard

FRANCES LINCOLN LIMITED
PUBLISHERS

ACKNOWLEDGMENTS

There are some parts of England that have a built-in reputation. The Lakes have that of long-standing beauty; Stratford has Shakespeare; Cornwall contends with the Riviera. Let me argue that of them all, the counties of Northumberland and Durham are the jewels in the crown. Today, a vague sense of not quite having emerged from the Ice Age seems to hang over this corner of England. If I have done anything to dispel this myth I shall not have worked in vain. I should like to express my sincere thanks to all of the people who assisted me with the project; and as with any such book there must for various reasons be omissions and in this respect I would ask the reader's indulgence. I would, however, like to mention the following: Alnwick Castle Estates Office; Lady Allendale of Bywell Castle; Mike Simpson of Blenkinsopp Castle; Ben Hamida of Lumley Castle; Antony Bainbridge of Haughton Castle; Sir Hugh Blackett of Halton Castle; Lord Barnard of Raby Castle; Chillingham Castle Estates Office; Philip Davis of Yorkshire for his invaluable help with the sites; Sue Rennie from Perth, Australia; Gary Carven for the IT help; Don Bennett of Durham; Michael Brunström at Frances Lincoln and English Heritage.
Most important of all is the huge debt of gratitude I owe to Mag for her unstinting and selfless help in making this book what it is.

Northumberland Strongholds
Frances Lincoln Ltd, 4 Torriano Mews, Torriano Avenue, London NW5 2RZ
www.franceslincoln.com

ISBN: 978-0-7112-2985-3

Printed and bound in Singapore

9 8 7 6 5 4 3 2 1

CONTENTS

FOREWORD

Centuries of war on the Scottish Border probably made Northumberland the bloodiest county in England and account for the multitude of castles and other fortified buildings throughout the area. My family, the Percies, became the principal power here after acquiring Alnwick Castle in 1309, gained fierced reputations as warriors and kingmakers and, from their strongholds at Alnwick and Warkworth, marched into battle against the Scots and, on several (usually disastrous) occasions, against the English monarch.

Castles could protect tonwsfolk and support garrisons but outlying farms and villages also needed protection from the 'Border Reivers' and their constant incursions in search of sheep, valuables and revenge. The fortified farms, houses and towers that pepper this rugged landscape bear witness to a violent 'normality' in the lives of generations of Northumbrians.

Ed Geldard has taken a rich subject matter, provided some fascinating and informative commentary and illustrated this handsome volume with some wonderful and dramatic photographs. It is a valuable record of a turbulant region, and I, for one, am grateful to live in the comparative peace of twenty-first- rather than fourteenth- or fifteenth-century Northumberland!

The Duke of Northumberland

INTRODUCTION

But first you must master their language, their
dialect, proverbs and songs
Don't trust any clerk to interpret when they come
with the tale of their wrongs.
Let them know that you know what they're saying; let
them feel that you know what to say.
Yes, even when you want to go hunting, hear 'em out
if it takes you all day.
Rudyard Kipling, 'Norman and Saxon'

Castles

Before the advent of the castle, the English knew the importance of fortifications. During the Iron Age, the Ancient Britons used earthworks to fortify their hilltops for tribal defences such as those at Lordenshaws. The Romans dotted the countryside with military encampments and built the impressive chain of forts known as the Saxon shore forts.

Shortly before the Norman Conquest the word castle came into use in the English language to indicate a type of fortress that was then new in this country. The earliest form of castle was known as the motte-and-bailey, a simple construction made of earth and wood, which could be built in just a few weeks. The motte was a large conical mound with a flat top. The bailey was a simple enclosure with its own ditch. It was usually laid out so that any point would be within a bowshot of the tower.

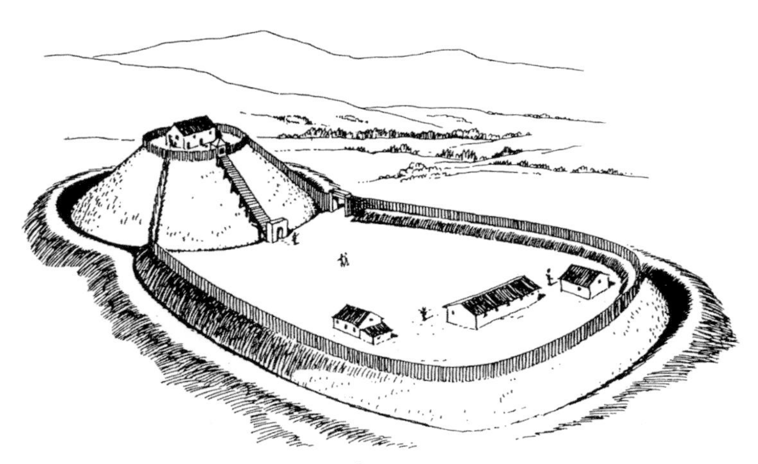

Motte & Bailey reconstruction

Inside the bailey were the living quarters, workshops and stables that were required to maintain the household in both war and peace. But if the lord and his retainers came under pressure they could withdraw into the keep and still be self-sufficient, although more austerely so. The ground floor of the keep was used as a storeroom; it also contained one of the most vital resources in times of siege, a well. The most important room within the keep was the Great Hall, the large living/eating room where the lord, his family and retainers would spend most of their time. The hall was, in most cases, two storeys high. This was to make sure that the smoke rising from the central hearth did not stifle the inhabitants. There was of course no chimney, and the fumes would gradually seep out through lateral holes in the roof. The lord and his family would be seated on a dais one or two steps above the rest of the hall; they also had a separate room, known as the solar, adjacent to the hall. All keeps would contain the essentials required for Norman life. These would include at least one chapel and a garderobe or latrine. This latter room would contain a stone seat above a shaft that lead down to a cesspit. It was not unknown for a castle to be taken by the opposition intrepid enough to climb through the shaft and risk the consequences in doing so.

Following the Battle of Hastings, the Normans consolidated their hold over England by rapidly constructing a large number of these castles. While such castles were quick and cheap to build, they suffered from a drawback. One of the materials used in the building of these castles was timber; it was perishable, and more importantly vulnerable to fire. A more durable medium was needed and that was stone, and once the early impetus of the Conquest had receded, the timber defences of motte-and-bailey castles were over time replaced by walls. From the earliest date, stone walls appear to have been crenellated, that is, they had battlements. These alternated along a wall with upright sections know as merlons.

During a siege, long before there was any question of gunpowder, both parties were able to call on artillery of one kind or another. The Roman arbalest was still in use at this time and could be adapted for missiles; its compactness and mobility made it useful for defence. Also available was 'Greek fire', a flaming substance unaffected by water; the formula was a secret handed down from one Byzantine emperor to the next for centuries and remains a mystery to this day. As one contemporary victim of Greek fire said to his comrades: 'Every time they hurl the fire at us, we go down on our elbows and knees, and beseech Our Lord to save us from this danger.'

By the end of the twelfth century, the castle was beginning to adopt the shape that we recognize today. For some five hundred years castles were of great importance in the defence of the realm; at times they were a matter of life and death. Their development reached its peak in the reign of Edward I. The Normans were prodigious builders. Not only did they erect massive stone castles but they also replaced most of the churches with equally commanding ecclesiastical edifices in stone. It can be safely said that their

Roman arbalest

great building drives of the late eleventh and early twelfth centuries were designed, in part, to impress their superior Norman technology and the permanence of their rule upon the English. As a result there are now more castles, bastles and pele towers in Northumberland than in any other county. The Domesday Book, which William the Conqueror had compiled in 1087, records a vast number of castles and defensible houses. In the survey of 1541, in which only part of the county was covered, no less than 120 castles were scheduled. Many have now disappeared, with many more reduced to ruins that are preserved by English Heritage. But even today there are still some sixty or seventy castles across Northumberland. Some of the most popular are Lindisfarne Castle, built on the orders of Henry VIII to protect from Scottish invasion, the ruins of Dunstanburgh, the largest castle in the country, and Bamburgh, from where the Angle kings once ruled the region.

Bates tells us that the survey of 1415 was probably completed in the early summer of that year. He suggests that it was done at the order of Henry V so that he knew about the security of his northern border before he embarked on his War with France; which ended in victory at Agincourt.

The 1541 survey, undertaken by Sir Robert Bowes and Sir Ralph Ellerker, was a Royal Commission from Henry VIII. In the sixteenth century it was rare for an English monarch to venture north of the Trent and Henry's desire to go further a field gave way to concern; following the 'Pilgrimage of Grace' revolt the north was somewhat unstable at the time. The visit, known as 'the progress', gave him an opportunity to meet his subjects. Planned since the early days of 1537 it wasn't to take place until the late summer of 1541. A 'progress' could last up to two months and usually took place between July and October. Carefully planned in advance the itinerary was set out in detailed tables called giests. Once the 'progress' was over the King would then return to London for the winter festivities. In Tudor times Christmas was a twelve-day festival with the climax of the celebrations reached on twelfth night. The advent fast came to an end on Christmas Eve; then followed twelve days of feasting, pageantry, 'guising' and merrymaking all presided over by the Lord of Misrule. Henry also observed the medieval custom of having a young man take the place of his most senior chaplain and play the role of bishop. By way of a contrast the Christmas of 1644 was a joyless time; for previous winters had been full of festive cheer and wild revelling and now not only had the puritan authorities denounced the celebrations as superstitious, but Christmas Day was on the same day as a compulsory public fast day.

Pele Towers and Bastles

If any Englishman steal in Scotland, or any Scotsman steal in England, any goods or cattels amounting to 12d [5p], he shall be punished by death.
Border Commissioners, 1605

From the time of Edward I, until the union of England and Scotland, the northern border of Northumberland was in a permanent state of warfare; for 400 years it was the scene of Border conflict. Feuding families, known as Border reivers, fought an endless series of raids in this Border region. Names such as Elliot, Armstrong, Charlton, Robson and Turnbull struck fear into the hearts of all around. The land on either side of the Anglo-Scottish border was each divided in to three areas: a West March, a Middle March and an East March, administered by a government official known as the 'Warden of the March'. These were part of the 'Debatable Land' that belonged to neither crown and where law ceased to exist. It was the Warden's duty to settle disputes among the residents of the march and to administer justice to the captured reivers. On both sides of the border most of the inhabitants belonged to a clan or family and if any member were in trouble the clan would come to their assistance. For over four hundred years these merciless reivers held sway over the most northerly part of England. The most prominent Border clans in the Debatable Land were the Armstrongs on the Scots side and the Grahams on the English. Regardless of place these cut-throats, brigands and cattle rustlers operated beyond the laws of England and Scotland. From the mid-sixteenth century, in response to Border raids by the reivers, wealthy farmers built a variant on the pele tower known as bastle houses. The word 'bastle' comes from the French 'bastille'. These two-storey fortified houses, built by farmers to protect their families and livestock, were unique to the Border region. In times of danger when the house would be under attack the stock would be barred in at the ground floor, while the family accessed the upper floor via a ladder and used the stone spout above the doorway for pouring hot liquids on to their attackers. A vaulted ground floor and stone staircase is a typical feature of these fortified dwellings. Some would view reivers as lovable rogues, while others saw them as mafia. Whatever your view their legacy remains in the fortified dwellings and their words; greenmail was the correct rent you paid, blackmail was for protection money. Peles were Gothic strongholds, the defences of which are earth mixed with timber, and strengthened with piles, such as those that were on the continent. Caesar describes them as the fortresses of the Britons. A pele tower is an old term used to describe fortified tower houses of between two and four storeys in height. Reverend Oliver Heslop, in *Northumberland Words: A Glossary of words in use in the County of Northumberland and on the Tyneside* (1892), defines a pele as

> a four-square tower used formerly for defence. The forms Peel Tower, Peel castle and Peel House are also used when speaking generally. The strongholds, nowadays called Peles are scattered over Northumberland, and present a similarity of type in construction and arrangement.

Although the north of the border knows them, the term is no longer used to describe these buildings in Northumberland. The only exception to this are the fortified towers built next to churches to provide protection for the priest; these are known as vicar's peles. They were occupied only in times of trouble and were built mainly in the Border areas of the North from the mid-fourteenth to the seventeenth century. Good examples of these can be seen at Corbridge (see page 24) and Elsdon (see page 26).

By the seventeenth century many of the castles had either disappeared or been abandoned; those that remained were becoming perilously close to ruin. Then came the English Civil War that gave them an inspired resurgence into their use; all over the country both Royalists and Parliamentarians held castles. Their remarkable defence of them proved to the country that there was 'life in the old dog yet'; however, this also was to prove their downfall. A victorious Parliament made certain that they would never again be in a position to pose a threat; they ordered most of them to be slighted, that is, damaged enough to make them useless for military use. Long after castles had lost their military usefulness they were to keep their appeal to the English as a residence.

Ed Geldard

River Tyne to River Coquet

AYDON CASTLE

A merchant by the name of Robert de Raymes built Castle as a private residence at the end of the thirteenth century; it is one of the finest fortified manor houses in England. Later it was to be owned by the Carnabys, who also owned Halton, the Carr's, the Collinsons and the Blacketts of Matfen. Situated above the deep wooded ravine of Cor Burn north of Corbridge, it can be reached by road or on foot. Its licence to crenellate was granted to Robert de Raymes in 1305, on the same day he was allowed to crenellate his mansion at Shortflatt; Edward I had illegally assumed the Scottish throne, and the need for its defence became apparent because of the ever-increasing lawlessness in the area.

The defences at Aydon are still extremely good. An outer wall, defended by arrow slits and turrets, encloses three courtyards, the inner of which gives access to the main building, cruciform in shape and two storeys high. From the smaller courtyard an outer staircase, which once had a roof, leads up to the entrance on the second floor. In the main part of the building is the Great Hall. Lit by two lancet windows separated by a decorated shaft and enclosed within a pointed arch, it overlooks the Dene.

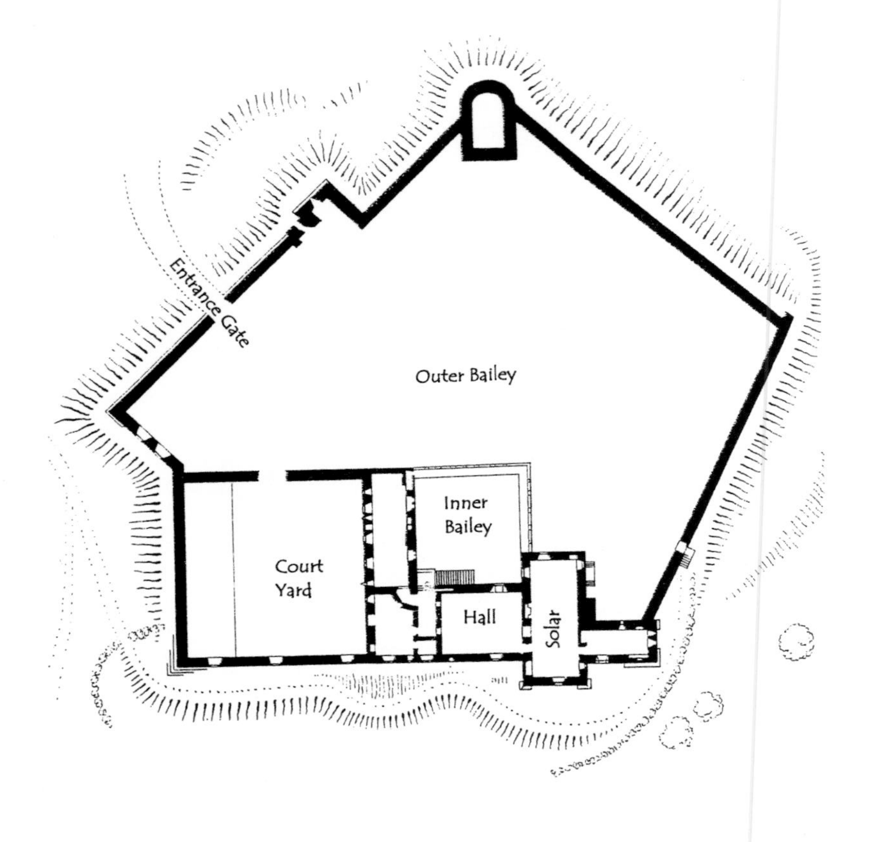

Divided from the hall by a screens passage, with a minstrels' gallery above, is the kitchen. The kitchen retains two original windows; in the sixteenth century the Carnaby family added the fireplace and on it carved their coat of arms. At the opposite end of the Great Hall a doorway leads to the 'solar' or private quarters. Below the Great Hall is a room with a fireplace projecting into the south wall, the chimney of which is one of the most remarkable features of the building. For almost half its height it has the normal appearance of a projecting chimney. It then becomes semi-circular and terminates in a cap, shaped like a cone, where lancet openings allow the smoke to escape.

In the barrel-vaulted basement of the west wing are the stables. At the edge of the Dene below the castle is a rock known as 'Jock's Leap'. According to legend, a Scottish-moss trooper, while being pursued by Sir Robert Clavering, escaped by leaping to this rock on the edge of the Dene while the rest of his party were being hurled from the cliff.

Many of the manor's owners were absent and leased the property to tenants; as a result it remained unchanged for centuries. In the seventeenth century the castle became a farmhouse and remained so until 1966; this has helped it to retain most of its features. No one will regret a visit to Aydon Castle; the building is in some respects unique.

BELSAY CASTLE

At Belsay we can see at once the transition from mansion house to castle. Along with Langley Castle (page 107) and Haughton Castle (page 29), it is perhaps the finest, as well as the most interesting, of all the single tower houses of Northumberland. Pevsner tells us that it is one of the most important sites in the whole country. It was built in the time of Edward II and is mentioned in the castle survey of 1415 as the 'Turris de Belsowe', belonging to one Johis Midilton. In the fourteenth century the family were temporarily divorced from the castle when Sir Gilbert Middleton quarrelled with the Crown after he held two cardinals and the bishop elect of Durham to ransom. The estates were then forfeit to the Crown and came into possession of Sir John Strivelyn. It was only when an ancestor of the Middleton family married the daughter of Sir John de Striveling that it was recovered. To this day it remains in the hands of the same family.

Square in plan and 60 feet in height, Belsay, like Chipchase Castle (page 22), is unique for its great corner bartizans, which overhang the corners on corbels. The bartizan in the south-west corner is higher than the others; this contains a newal stair. Both bartizans and battlements are embrasured, and the corbel parapets are at least two feet out from the walls and have machicolations for the delivery of missiles. Formerly the walls were decorated similar to those at Bothal Castle (see page 19) with shields carved with coats of arms, and may have been similarly surmounted by stone figures. The basement is tunnel vaulted. The Hall above has finely balanced windows, of which one is traceried. A wing added to the tower in the seventeenth century bears the following inscription: 'Thomas Middleton and Dorothy his wife built this house 1614' and beneath are the Middleton coat of arms with those of Strivelyn; this was to signify the loyalty between the two families. Sir Charles Monck, who had changed his name from Middleton in order to satisfy the terms of his maternal grandfather's will, built Belsay Hall in the early nineteenth century to his own design; the young architect John Dobson drew up the plans. Sir Charles, a lover of Grecian architecture, brought workmen from Greece to build his new home. The honey-coloured sandstone with which the mansion is built was quarried from the grounds at the back.

BLACK MIDDENS BASTLE

Set in the walking country of North Tynedale, the bastle at Black Middens is of a type that is seldom seen in the Borders; its ground floor had a timber ceiling instead of a vaulted stone roof. It still preserves its upper storey and original entrance, the lintel of which has sockets for three iron bars. The window to the left of it had at one time square wooden bars. In times of danger, when reivers might be around, stock would be barred in at the ground floor, while the family accessed the upper floor via a ladder, which would be drawn up behind them.

BLENKINSOPP CASTLE

All round Haltwhistle are the remains, or the sites, of fortresses; Bellister (see page 94) is a ruin, 4 miles to the west is Thirlwall (see page 39), and finally Blenkinsopp. It was here at Blenkinsopp, on 4 February 1340, that Thomas de Blencansopp was granted a licence to crenellate his manor house. This licence was confirmed on 11 May. The fruition of this licence was a square tower with a vaulted basement and walls 7 feet in thickness, defended by a ditch on the north and west sides, on the south by the Tipalt Burn and on the east by a steep bank. The historian Hodgson tells us, 'The old family residence stood on the right bank of the hope or valley of Glenwhelt; prior to the Conquest it had probably belonged to one Blencan, from whom the place and township derived its name, for in the oldest writings it is called Blencan or Blenkens-hope.' However, the Blenkinsopps were to desert it about 1490 in favour of Bellister. In the 1541 survey, Sir Robert Bowes had this to say: 'At Blenkinsoppe ys a toure of thinherytaunce of John Blenkinsoppe and is decayee in the roofe and not in good rep'ac'ons.'

It was to be rebuilt in the Gothic style by William Glover in 1877–80, but sadly a fire in 1954 gutted this building and only the east wall and part of the curtain wall survived.

Though the castle has seen many changes, the ghost of the White Lady remains; she wanders disconsolately through the castle trying to tell someone of the vault with the chest of gold she had hidden from her husband. According to tradition, Bryan de Blenkinsopp was overheard to say that he would never marry unless his bride was so wealthy that it would take ten men to carry her dowry of gold into the castle; and sure enough some time after he was to bring back from the Crusades a wife and a large chest of gold. Unfortunately the lady soon realized that she had been married for her money and hid it within the castle grounds. Aggrieved by his wife's behaviour he immediately left the castle and was never to be heard of again. The lady was inconsolable and set out with her attendants in search of him, but he was never to return. It is said the lady, filled with remorse, cannot rest in her grave until someone will follow her to the vault and release her soul.

On the opposite side of the valley is Blenkinsopp Hall, built by John Blenkinsopp Coulson. Not to be outdone by the castle there is a tradition of a black dog here, which appears as a warning of a coming death; it then reappears at the moment of dissolution.

BOTHAL CASTLE

Not far from Pegsworth is the lovely village of Bothal. This tiny place centres on its Saxon church, and its name, derived from 'bottell', means abode. The castle here, overlooking the River Wansbeck, has stood on this site since Saxon times. The design, like that of Dunstanburgh, is simply that of an elongated bailey enclosed by a curtain wall and entered by a fortified gateway. Mentioned as early as 1166, it came to William Bertram, Baron of Mitford, by marriage.

The year 1343 was a major date in the Castle's development; for it was then that Roger Bertram received from Edward III his licence to crenellate; after his death the castle then passed, through the marriage of his heiress daughter, into the hands of the Ogle family. It was then that the gatehouse keep was built, the great hall enlarged and the curtain wall strengthened. In 1410, a family dispute led to Sir Robert Ogle laying siege to the castle, which was then occupied by his brother, Sir John Ogle. The siege, carried out with 200 men-at-arms and archers, continued for four days until a sheriff's proclamation was read out at the castle gates. It stated that 'Sir Robert Ogle and all other people abiding therein should be put out without delay upon pain of forfeiture of life and members'. An intervention by the King saw the return of the castle to Sir John Ogle. In 1672 Rector Booth of Bothal Church was caught in the castle ruins melting down coins of the realm; 200 years later workmen found a block of silver thought to have been hidden there by Booth's wife.

If there was a motte, it has now disappeared beneath the restored gatehouse tower. The gatehouse, rectangular in shape, has an admirable display of heraldry both on and below the merlons; these bear the arms of the Black Prince, Edward III, Percy Bertram, Darcy, Conyers and Felton. Those of Edward III on the central merlon show the leopards of England coming before the lilies of France; this is very rare in this form. The role of the figures on the battlements is twofold, as well as being decorative they are also meant to deceive: to delude attackers that there was a permanent watch, as at Alnwick (see page 49). On the central merlon is a stone figure holding a horn or musical instrument, while on the north-west turret, a second figure is in the act of hurling down a stone. The entrance passage itself has a ribbed and pointed barrel-vault, with three blocked meutrieres, or murder holes, in the roof for surprising any invaders. Only one or two of the original fourteenth-century windows survive at first-floor level. The transomed Perpendicular window and drawing room fireplace were both brought from Cockle Park Tower. Gardens and orchards now fill the space that lies beyond the gatehouse and within the curtain wall.

BYWELL CASTLE

Bywell Castle 1786
From a sketch by S.H. Grimm

A castle has stood here since the early twelfth century, soon after the death of Guy de Balliol. It stands sited on a double bend, not far from a river crossing on the north bank of the Tyne. Its earliest mention is in 1464 when Henry VI chose to hide here after the Battle of Hexham, which was to bring to a close a phase in the War of the Roses that had begun in 1459; its aftermath saw the death or exile of all the leading Lancastrians and left Edward IV in undisputed control of the kingdom.

Although the castle is roofless the shell remains largely intact and is made up of three interconnecting structures: a gatehouse, a curtain wall and the house itself. The entrance to the south-facing gatehouse is by way of an arched gate passage, which is flanked on either side by plain barrel-vaulted chambers. On the west side of the passage is a door leading to the stair, which was protected by a 'yett', or door reinforced by a complicated iron grill with overlapping bars. At the top of the stair is a murder hole through which to attack intruders from above. A newel stair gives access to the upper floors and battlements. Extending eastward from the gatehouse, a long section of the curtain wall still survives. By the seventeenth century the castle had been robbed of its lead and the timbers were in decay; the fisheries were being poached and the dam broken. Finally, after being in the hands of the Crown for a number or years, the estate was sold to the Fenwicks of Fenwick Tower (see page 123). In 1820 it was to exchange hands once more and was purchased by the Beaumonts.

CAMBO PELE

The beautiful village of Cambo lies on a ridge to the north of the Newcastle to Otterburn road. The village was formerly a staging station on the old coach road that came this way from Belsay, then passed Winter's Gibbet and on to Otterburn. In 1740 Sir Walter Blackett began to develop the small village of Camhoe into a model village; its rows of quite and secluded houses, half hidden by flowers, are away from the main road. The oldest building is the post office, formerly a sixteenth-century tower house. It is referred to in the book *In Troublesome Times: Cambo Women's Institute* (1922): Mr George Handyside, then tenant of the tower, said, 'My father and grandfather had this shop before me and before them it was kept by a warlock [wizard] and people daursn't owe him anything.' That would have been in about 1814. The date of 1818 on a window lintel records when the pele was altered to make it more habitable. In the centre of the village is the 'dolphin' fountain built by Sir Charles Edward Trevelyan as part of the remodelling of the village.

CHIPCHASE CASTLE

Looking southwards across one of the most beautiful stretches of the North Tyne Valley, Chipchase Castle lies a mile and a half to the south-east of Wark. It is a mixture of medieval pele and Jacobean manor. Dating back to Saxon times, its name is derived from the old English word cheap, meaning a market, and the French word chasse, a hunting ground. Its history goes back to the reign of Henry II, when it was a hunting ground owned by the Lords of Prudhoe, the great Umfravilles. It was they who built a small fort to defend the village that existed then, then later built the tower that now forms so striking a part of the building. With the marriage of Cecily de Lisle to Walter Heron in 1348 the manor passed to the Herons of Ford. In 1621 Cuthbert Heron merged the impressive Jacobean manor house with the old pele tower. The Herons also played a crucial part in Border affairs. Twenty-eight years before the union, Sir George Heron, keeper of Tynedale and High Sheriff of Northumberland, was slain in one of the last Border skirmishes at Reidswire. The last of the Herons of Chipchase was Sir Harry, who sold the castle and estate to John Reed in 1727. In his *Comprehensive Guide to Northumberland* (1888), W.W. Tomlinson tells of a subterranean passage used in times of siege from the cellar to the site of the ancient village of Chipchase.

COCKLAW TOWER

Cocklaw lies in the North Tyne Valley 4 miles north of Hexham, near Chollerton. The tower here is typical of the dozens of strongholds built in the fifteenth century. The pele is large and substantial, measuring about 40 × 50 feet and the height on the east side is still 35 feet. Less important than Haughton or Chipchase, but larger than many of its kind, it is a good example of a Border keep. Built by the Errington family more than 600 years ago, it was their home for nearly 200 years before they came into possession of the much more spacious castle of Beafront near Hexham. Although there is now no longer evidence of other buildings around the tower, there are records of a chapel. Traces of frescoes can be seen on the south walls of the principal apartment in which the family lived. This is a Grade I listed building.

CORBRIDGE VICAR'S PELE

On the north bank of the Tyne, some 17 miles west of Newcastle, lies the attractive town of Corbridge. In 1830, Hodgson had this to say:

> The town (for such its antiquity demands that it be styled) is dirty, and in all the streets except which the Newcastle and Carlisle road passes, is filthy with middens and pigsties, with railing before them of split boards etc. The population seems half-fed; the women sallow, thin-armed, and the men flabby, pot-bellied and tender-footed; but still the place bears the appearance of being ancient.

The vicar's pele was rected at the beginning of the fourteenth century on the south side of the churchyard. Built for the protection of the church during Scottish raids, it became known as 'the Lord's gaol'. This three-storey fortified tower still retains its old thick wooden door lined with iron bars. From the vaulted basement, where the vicar must have stabled his horse, a stair mounts in the thickness of the wall to the upper rooms. The west front has one small window that allows light to fall on a stone book-rest where past vicars of Corbridge must have contemplated their sermons.

The stones which built it are Roman, brought probably from the nearby ruins of Corstopitum.

CRESSWELL TOWER

This fine example of an ancient pele stands close to the sea, at the south end of Druridge Bay, one of the most beautiful stretches of sand on the Northumberland coast. The Cresswells had their seat here since the time of Richard I, when Robert de Cresswell was in possession of a manor. This hoary old tower also has its ghost. A legend of the Cresswell family takes us back to Saxon times. 'The White Lady of Cresswell' was, according to legend, the daughter of one of the old Barons of Cresswell. Standing one day on the turret of the old tower, she suffered a terrible vision of seeing her lover, a Danish prince, slain on the seashore by her three brothers. She was so stricken with grief that she refused to eat, and starved to death.

The tower was recently conserved to prevent it falling into further ruin. This is a now a Scheduled Monument protected by law.

ELSDON VICAR'S PELE

Set in rugged moorland, the village of Elsdon lies secluded 3 miles to the east of Otterburn; in 1249, it was the capital of the remote Middle March. Dominating the village is the tower; for some 500 years it has withstood weather and foe alike. It was one of the Norman Umfravilles who built it, and their arms, showing a cinquefoil and eight crosses supported by two wolves each bearing a sword upright, can be found on the south wall.

The pele tower is the rectory and some of the rectors of Elsdon have been men of eminence. The Rev. C. Dodgson, afterwards Bishop of Ossery, incumbent from 1762–5 wrote:

> The vestibule of the castle is a low stable, and above it is the kitchen, in which there are two little beds joining to each other. The curate and his wife lay in one, and Margery, the maid, in the other. I lay in the parlour, between two beds, to keep me from being frozen to death, for, as we keep open house, the winds enter from every quarter, and are apt to creep into bed to one.

A high wall round the garden represents the old barmkin, a defence essential to an area so near to the Border.

GREAT TOSSEN TOWER, ROTHBURY

The remains of Great Tossen Tower lie at the eastern end of the hamlet in the Upper Coquet Valley, opposite a farmhouse that was formerly the Royal George Inn. Originally the Hepple family held it, then the Tailbois and finally the Ogles. Sir Robert Bowes, in the Border survey of 1541, made the comment 'At Great Tossen is a tower of the lorde Ogle's Inherytance not in good rep'ac'ons'. The site commands an extensive view northwards across the Coquet Valley and as such it was one of a line of towers that stretched from Harbottle to Warkworth. It was an excellent vantage point for detecting reivers. However the tower today, as it raises its ragged walls to the sky, is of no great consequence. It has been robbed of its building stone, but the ashlar has been left at the higher levels and the walls, almost 9 feet thick, consist mainly of rubble. The vaulted basement would have served for storage. Access to the upper floors was by the newel stair at the entrance. A fireplace on the north side heated the hall on the first floor. At its north-east corner the hall also had a garderobe. From the hall the stair would have continued up to the second floor, which would have housed the solar, and there would almost certainly have been an embattled parapet similar to that at Cocklaw (see page 23). The nearby spring, thought to have been inside the barmkin wall, now flows only in wet weather.

In 1517 William Ogle gave Tossen Tower to Lord Ogle in exchange for Cocklaw Tower near Haughton.

HALTON TOWER, CORBRIDGE

Lying half a mile north of Aydon Castle (see page 14) is the tower at Halton, which is impressive enough to warrant the name of castle. Standing four floors high with corbelled turrets at its corners, it really comprises of three buildings: a pele tower of the de Halton family, a picturesque manor house and a charming Jacobean house. The delightful garden adds to the aspect of this historic place.

Like so many of their day, if an opportunity of reiving arose, the de Haltons were more than likely to join in. In 1276, Sir John Halton, then the Sheriff of Northumberland, was drawn into a futile raid at Wark on Tyne. He was caught in the act of 'lifting' cattle belonging to one Thomas Fairburn of Wark on Tyne, and then had to suffer the disgrace of being brought before his own court. The evidence was so strong that his own court could not avoid pronouncing him guilty. By paying the aggrieved party a trifling ten marks he escaped going to prison. The last of the de Haltons died in 1345 and shortly afterwards the manor passed into the hands of the Carnabys when a male member of their family married the daughter of John de Halton.

HAUGHTON CASTLE

Haughton Castle sits in an area well known for its salmon and trout fishing, and the most striking view of it is from either side of the river, where an old ferry used to run. An agreement to operate the ferry was drawn up between Ranulf de Havelton and William de Swynburne during the reign of Henry II.

The first recorded owner of the manor was Ranulf, son of Huctred, who gave it through the marriage of his daughter to one Reginald Pratt, Lord of Knaredale and Esquire to William of Scotland. The grandson of Reginald then sold off all his lands in Haughton to William de Swyneburne, treasurer to the Scottish Queen, and it is he who erected the castle, which dates from the thirteenth century. It is first mentioned as a castle in 1373, when the walls had been massively strengthened and the building crenellated, and, in spite of belonging to the Swyneburns, it was entered in the list of 1415 as being the 'castrum' of one John de Widdrington. The de Widdringtons were then to hold it for several centuries.

Haughton's history is a turbulent one, as were many of the Border strongholds, and like all castles it has a ghost. The story relates to the days when the reivers, or mosstroopers,

Haughton Castle in 1538
From a sketch at the Record Office

would carry out their attacks on English land, which was then quite legal, before they returned to Scotland. In 1541 the Armstrongs attacked the castle and made off with nine horses and forty pounds; Sir John de Widdrington was at the time Lord of Haughton. Archie Armstrong, who was the chief of his clan, was caught by Sir Thomas de Swyneburn and flung into the dungeon at Haughton.

It was at this point that Lord Cardinal Wolsey summoned Sir Thomas to York to report on Lord Dacre of Gisland, who

had been colluding with the Armstrongs; when he was well on his way he became aware of a large key hanging from his belt. With dismay he remembered the reiver whom he'd imprisoned three days previously without food or water, and being a humane man was struck by the horrendous consequences of his neglect. Without seeing the Cardinal, he turned his horse and returned at speed back to Haughton. As he reached Durham his horse collapsed and died beneath him; but by borrowing another (it is always two or three in the best stories) he arrived at the castle gate exhausted two days later. On reaching the dungeon deep in the depths of the castle his worst fears were confirmed: Archie Armstrong was dead. Maddened by hunger he had gnawed the flesh from his arms. In the years that followed servants were afraid of working in the castle, believing that the shrieks of Archie Armstrong could still be heard coming from the dungeon. The rector from nearby Simonburn was called and, aided by a black bible, he was able to exorcise the ghost. The screams were heard again some years later when the bible was taken away for repair; quickly the bible was returned and the shrieking stopped. Local legend tells us that the screams can still be heard whenever a descendant of Sir John sets foot inside the castle. Once described as being 'chiefly dismantled with few apartments remaining habitable', it is hard to believe that the castle of today is the result of careful rebuilding over the years by its various owners.

Originally it was one of the better class of tower house not unlike Langley Castle (see page 107) but having more ambitious lines with five square turrets to break the line of the battlements; the barmkin is now gone. A drawing of 1538 shows the barmkin and gateway to the south, and in dry weather traces of the barmkin appear on the lawns. Outside, there is the unique feature of five blind bay arcades of tall pointed arches in the north and south fronts; meutrieres in the soffits protect the wall feet. Over the past two centuries the interior has changed but it still retains the twin segmental vaults that run the length of the building; a second entrance was created above and a newal stair led to the wall-walk in the south-west turret. Two of the rooms have Jacobean over-mantels taken from a house in the Sandhill area of Newcastle. The north side of the castle, relieved with corbelled garderobes, is the most picturesque.

On Tuesday 13 November 1860, at 2 p.m., the castle and its contents went to auction. It was described as 'a relic of the thirteenth century, but suitable for the Residence of a Gentleman's family, and having Walled Gardens, Offices, Lodge, Lawns, Ornamental Shrubberies and a well-stocked Fish Pond; is romantically situated upon the brink of the North Tyne'. The asking price was £3-2s-7p.

HORSLEY TOWER, LONGHORSLEY

The rugged old pele tower at Longhorsley forms a striking landmark on the road to Rothbury 6 miles from Morpeth. There does not seem to be any record of its building; it is not mentioned in the lists made in 1415 or 1541, but it is known to have been built by the Horsley family. The huge pele of four storeys measures some 42 × 32 feet.

There is an entrance on the east side, and an old square-headed doorway in the south wall has been changed into a window. This leads to the barrel-vaulted ground floor where a newal stair in the south-east corner takes us to the roof. At its eastern end are two smaller rooms, one of which leads to a seventeenth-century wing and the 'Lady's Room'. The three upper floors hold little of interest apart a fireplace with stone lintel on the first floor, which was found here when some of the wall panelling was removed. And although they still retain their original hood-moulds, all the windows have been replaced. The crenellated battlements, because of their height, appear to have been designed for ornamentation rather than that of defence, and there is a walk around the battlements from which fine views of the village are to be seen. From the Horsleys the tower passed into the hands of the Riddells of Swinburn, and for many years it was the residence of a priest. It is now owned privately.

MITFORD CASTLE

There were Mitfords here in Saxon times, but it was not until the arrival of William the Conqueror that a stronghold was built here when he gave the hand of Sybil de Mitford to Richard Bertram. The Bertram family were to hold the estates until 1264, when the rebellious Roger took up arms against Henry III and forfeited them all to the Crown. Built some time between 1066 and 1100 by William Bertram, the castle stands on a rocky ridge on the south bank of the Wansbeck. The site was well chosen: the Wansbeck guarded the motte on one side, steep slopes on the others, while an encircling moat could be fed from the river. The castle also guarded the ford across the river. A footpath leads from the bridge up to the castle. The gatehouse to the outer ward was apparently on the east side, but all traces of the entrance itself have now vanished. Beyond the north wall are the remains of a gateway that led to the barmkin. At the beginning of the thirteenth century a stone keep of five sides was built within the inner ward; this is the only five-sided keep in England. The crumbling walls of the keep still reach upward, but little is left of the curtain wall that once encircled this steep knoll. King John was to sack it in 1216 during his dispute with the barons, and it was to suffer further at the hands of Scots. In 1315 it was the headquarters of Gilbert de Middleton who, in one of his get-rich-quick schemes, abused his position as a Warden of the March; he began to fill the dungeons at Mitford with prisoners, whom he held to ransom. However, his career was to come to an abrupt end when he kidnapped the Bishop of Durham and his brother. Having taken them by surprise at Rushyford, some 6 miles south of Durham, Middleton then held the Bishop in Morpeth and brought his brother to Mitford. It was William de Felton who raised the ransom asked for, and on the appointed day he went to see Middleton to report that the money was being held in the village. Middleton was to renege on the deal that he had struck, and as they left the castle a band of his own men set about killing the party. In the ensuing affray both Gilbert and John Middleton were captured and taken to London for execution.

In the early fourteenth century, Eleanor, widow of Henry III, was to grant Mitford to Eleanor de Geneva, recently married to one Robert de Stuteville. Then John de Stuteville gave it to Aymer de Valence, Earl of Pembroke; who had the misfortune to be slain at a tournament held in celebration of his wedding. And as strong as the castle may have been it existed for only a brief time; by 1327 it was described as the 'site of a castle wholly burned' and was dismantled to prevent it being used by the Northumbrian barons that were in league with the Scots. Excavations in the late 1930s were to reveal that an early Norman graveyard lay under a chapel; in plan it is not unlike the chapel that is in Warkworth Castle (see page 41).

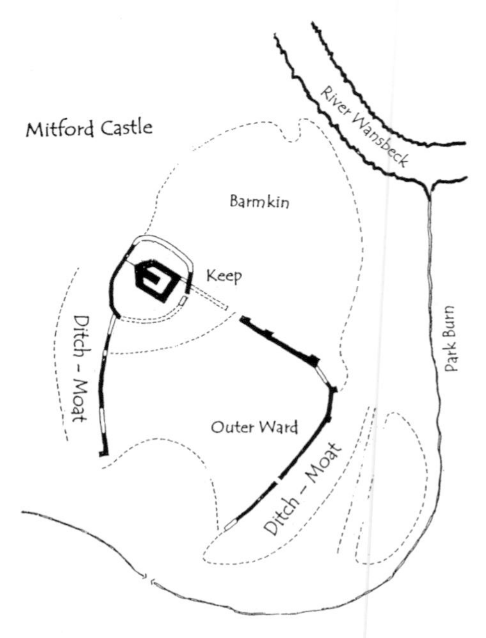

MORPETH CASTLE

There have been two castles at Morpeth; the first was on Castle Hill and the second on Ha' Hill. Of the castle built following the Conquest little now remains and the early history of the present castle is not easy to follow because every time it is referred to there is some uncertainty about which castle is being described; like that of its predecessor, it also was strengthened by a ditch. From the first it may have consisted solely of a walled enclosure and gatehouse, like those of Dunstanburgh and Bothal. The site on Ha' Hill is assumed to have been the site where William de Merlay built his castle after being granted the Barony of Morpeth. Its first mention is in the latter part of the eleventh century as being a small fortress. It is referred to again in connection with the abbey at Newminster when, in 1138, Ranulph de Merlay entertained here eight monks from Fountains Abbey; he had invited them north to found a new monastery. Then, in 1216, King John was to burn the castle in his revenge against the barons for rebelling. After Henry III restored their estates in 1218 the Merlays were to build their castle on the southern side of the burn. Of the castle only the gatehouse and part of the curtain wall now remains. The gatehouse, with its tunnel vault and four-centred arches lies at the north end of the east wall. Within the vaulted roof of the passage there is the outline of a meurtriere used to surprise attackers. It is interesting to note there is no portcullis here. At the time of the Union of England and Scotland the castle was beginning to fall into disrepair, and ironically the fortress that had survived the Border Wars was to fall during the Civil War. It was garrisoned at that time by a force of 500 men when it came under attack from the Marquis of Montrose and his army of 2,700 men. In a siege that lasted twenty days, the garrison lost twenty-three men to Montrose's 191; it was surrendered on terms to the Marquis. At one point in the siege Montrose was to move his cannon to a better position where he was successful in breaching the walls; however, the breach was short-lived for it was promptly closed with feather beds. The trenches thrown up by the attacking forces may still be seen to the west of the castle. The estates were then to pass by marriage though a number of families until they came to the possession of the infamous 'Belted' Will Howard of Naworth Castle. Lord Howard at this time was known to have kept a small garrison at Naworth, to hold in check the marauding of the moss troopers whom he punished with the utmost severity. The chronicler Fuller tells us 'when at their greatest height the moss troopers had two enemies, the laws of the land and Lord William Howard of Naworth'.

A royal visitor to Morpeth Castle was the Tudor Princess Margaret, who was to become the wife of James IV. The widowed queen, after the tragedy of Flodden, went on to marry the Earl of Angus and gave birth to a daughter at the castle of Harbottle. She was moved by litter first to Carrington Castle and then to Morpeth, the castle of Lord Dacre.

NEWCASTLE CASTLE

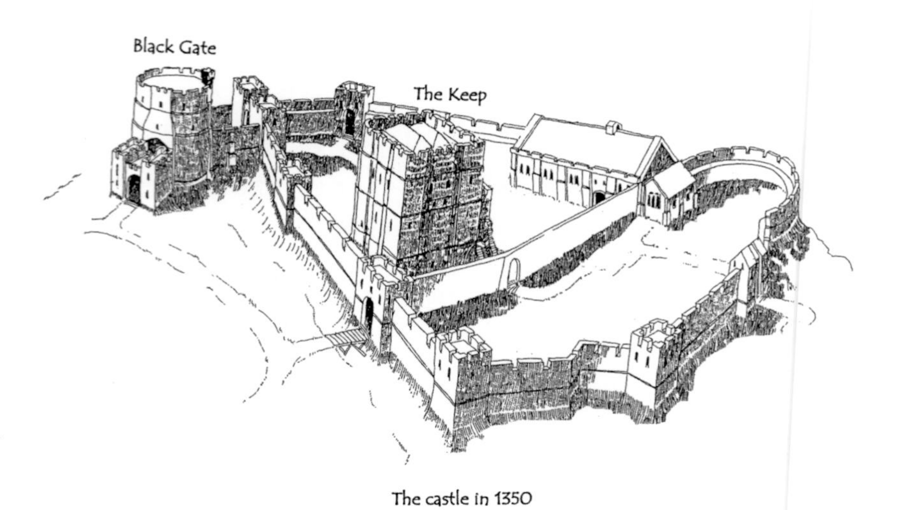

The castle in 1350

Newcastle owes its importance to its foundation on the River Tyne and its easy access to the sea. The Emperor Hadrian, of the Aelius family, was the first to realise this importance and bridged the narrow steep sided valley of the Tyne, defending its northern bank with a small fort known as 'Pons Aelius'.

Our first knowledge of a medieval castle on this site, which gave the town its name, is before the conquest. Symeon of Durham tells us that in 1080 William I sent his illegitimate son Robert on an expedition against Scotland. It was on his return from that journey that he was to erect a stockade on this site, hence, as Speed has it, 'laid the foundation of a castle whereby the town of Newcastle did afterwards both take her beginning and her name'. Robert's castle would have been of the usual motte and bailey type, but exact details of it are now unknown. This type of defence was brought in by the Norman knights, whom Edward the Confessor had sent to defend Hereford against the inroads of the Welsh.

The present building dates from the time of Henry II. In 1155 he was to resume possession of all castles and other royal households in Northumberland, and ordered the destruction of any unlicensed strongholds that arose during the civil wars of the previous reign. This highhanded manner, along with his resumption of the Earldom of Northumberland, made him realise the resentment felt by Scotland, and with this in mind, the importance of increasing the frontier defences of his kingdom. Newcastle featured in these defences because it commanded the road crossing at the River Tyne, and for centuries it had been one of the main arteries of communication between the two countries. It would appear from the pipe rolls that in 1172 a stone castle, taking five years to build at a cost of £911-10s-9d, would replace this wooden structure. Built by the first Plantagenet, the keep shows the transition from late Norman architecture to the early Gothic, of which the Black Gate is an example. The curtain walls of the north and south baileys have not survived except on the riverside to the south,

where the castle walls stand on the edge of a steep slope that leads down to the quayside. Today steep stairs that descend from the postern gate enable us to make this journey. Almost square in shape it measures some 62 × 56 feet, excluding the fore building. Square projections are at three of the corners, and an irregular polygonal tower stands at the north-west to make the fourth. The walls at the base were deliberately splayed so that any liquid poured down from the battlements would be diverted against the attackers at the foot of the wall. An external staircase on the east side of the fore building leads to the entrance; the small niche on either side of the stair is for oil lamps used to light the entrance at night. Each floor of the keep has one principal room with minor rooms off it; these are set in the thick walls. On the south side of the Great Hall, in the thickness of the wall, is the barrel-vaulted 'King's Chamber'. It is skilfully sited under the two southern windows in the Great Hall so that both rooms may enjoy the sun. The castle also had its own provision for religion by having a chapel to occupy the whole of the basement below the fore building; its rib vaulting gives a good idea of the ecclesiastical architecture of the Normans at that time. For almost 200 years it was a common gaol, then in 1644 the keep was involved in its last fight with the Scots; Sir John Marley surrendered two days after the rest of the town had fallen. In medieval times Newcastle was a walled town; walls built during the reign of Edward I were subject to a wall tax paid by the Burgesses. Edward III was to fine it for not maintaining its walls even though the tax was collected.

The Black Gate dates from the middle of the thirteenth century. It was a formidable addition to the castle wall when built in 1248. With the exception of Dunstanburgh, this is one of the best examples of a gatehouse in the county, and one of the finest in all England. It is by way of a barbican before the main gate of the castle and its position in the west wall enabled sentries to monitor this section of the wall. The ground plan is simplicity itself: a central passage flanked by twin towers contains the guardrooms. The towers, however, are not only projections; they flank the whole gateway in a wide outward curve. The gateway is in three parts: an outer with portcullis, the middle gate and a vaulted inner section; grooves show where the portcullis was, and where the open meutrieres in the roof were, from which the enemy, held up by the gates, could be attacked. Beyond the gatehouse lay the drawbridge that spanned a dry moat; it was not until this point that the attackers could reach the north gate and force their way into the castle bailey.

The gate is said to derive its name from Patrick Black, a tenant in the time of James I. However, by the middle of the nineteenth century it had been reduced to slum dwellings accommodating twelve families and a public house. It was not until 1855, as engineers cut through the castle ward to clear old property for the new railway line, that the building emerged from the huddle of houses that had surrounded it. Strong opposition prevented not only its demolition but also stopped any new buildings that would have destroyed the picturesque nature of the site. In 1883 the Society of Antiquaries became interested in the two-storey house that surmounts the Black Gate; it was to then lease the property and spend over £1,600 in renovating it. The Society still occupies the building to this day, using it as a meeting place and library.

OTTERBURN TOWER

The name Otterburn, recalling the most famous of all Border frays – one fought under a bright moon in August 1388 – is now more famed for its tweed and woollen goods. The battle brought together Sir Henry Percy, known as Harry 'Hotspur', and James, Earl of Douglas. Froissart tells us that the Scottish army, while awaiting the arrival of Earl Percy and his forces, tried to take the tower. At first victory seemed to lean toward the English; dismayed at seeing his men repulsed, Douglas seized a battle-axe and dashed into the middle of the affray. Pierced by three spears, he fell to the ground fatally wounded. By the beginning of the fifteenth century the tower was in the possession of Sir Robert Umfraville; it was later to pass into the hands of the Halls, one of the clans in Redesdale. Its most famous owner was 'Mad Jack Hall', a well-known Jacobite rebel. Reprieved five times when tried for high treason he was eventually executed at Tyburn Hill. At his trial he pleaded that as he returned from a justices' meeting he was surrounded by rebels and forced to go with them. His initials are still to be seen above one of the original doors.

PONTELAND TOWER BLACKBIRD INN

Ponteland tower is one of those Border strongholds that, like a phoenix rising from the ashes, received a new lease of life. The Blackbird Inn now forms part of an old tower house where peace between England and Scotland was negotiated in 1244. In the next century it was to take part in the events that lead up to the most celebrated of Border frays. The Scottish army on its march to Otterburn burnt both town and castle. Froissart's description of the incident reads:

> On the morrow, the Scots dislodged from before Newcastle; and, taking the road to their own country, they came to a castle and town called Pontclau, of which a very valiant knight of Northumberland was the lord. They halted there about four o'clock in the morning, as they learned the knight to be within it, and made preparations for the assault. This was done with such courage that the place was won, and the knight made prisoner. After they had burned the town and castle, they marched away to Otterburn.

The basement of the tower is vaulted and the entrance is on the north side by a narrow weatherworn door. Overhead is a meutriere, through which hot liquids could be poured in an emergency. Mark Errington, whose initials appear above a first floor window, restored and extended the house in the sixteenth century. During the seventeenth century it fell into ruins and was roofless until 1935; once restored it became an inn.

PONTELAND VICAR'S PELE

Ponteland is a small village on the River Ponte from which it takes its name. In the rectory garden stands a medieval tower that Pevsner describes as 'the ruins of a Tower House'. It is entered as 'turris de Ponteland' in the listing of 1415 and being then the property of 'vicar eiusdem'. According to local legend at one time there ran a secret passage from the cellars to Ponteland Tower. The construction is of rough coursed stone and there is evidence that it once had three storeys. At the base of a blocked first floor doorway is part of a medieval grave cover incised with a Celtic cross. Remains of a basement vault and a mural stair can be seen in the north wall, where a blocked first floor doorway reuses a twelfth-century cross slab in its jamb.

THIRLWALL CASTLE

The shattered remains of Thirlwall Castle stand close to the Roman wall 3½ miles west of Haltwhistle. Entirely built of stones from the nearby Roman station at Magna, this grim stronghold of the Thirlwalls is situated on high ground above the river. We first hear of Thirlwall in 1255 when it was part of Scotland, its name being derived from 'a breach in the wall'. At that time the prioress of the nearby nunnery had allowed her cattle on to land claimed by the Baron of Thirlwall. Their argument was to grow so heated that eventually she challenged him to combat in order to settle the matter once and for all. This was not as funny as it may sound since it was the custom for disputants to hire champions to fight for them. The arrangements had almost been made for the tourney, when the Prioress agreed against her will to pay ten pounds for any damage her animals may have caused; she then had to pay a further twenty shillings for inciting a shepherd to burn down a house on the Baron's estate. The castle is mentioned in both surveys and was described in 1541 as 'being in measurable good reparations' when held by Robert Thirlwall. After the Union of the English and Scottish Crowns, Border strongholds became redundant in their use and after 300 years the family were to abandon it at the beginning of the seventeenth century. In 1748 the Howards of Naworth purchased the Thirlwall estates for £4,000; Lord Howard, being only interested in the land, allowed the castle to fall into decay. In its day, the castle consisted of a main block with a tower on the east side, and from the entrance a newel stair, in the thickness of the wall, went up to the turret. The south wall is now gone, most of it in Tipalt Burn, while the north-east towers and corners have squared quoins.

The castle is not without its ghost story. Legend tells us of a Baron of Thirlwall who returned from a Border raid carrying with him a table of solid gold. In time the Scots attacked the castle and the Baron with his retainers slain; the Scots then began their search for the treasure, which was in the care of a mysterious dwarf. In the heat of the fray the dwarf threw himself and the treasure into a well. Then, by supernatural power, he drew the top down over himself and his charge. And there he remains, still under the influence of the spell, until the son of a widow releases him from it.

TYNEMOUTH CASTLE

This castle, standing at the neck of a promontory, once served as a protection for the monastery that lay behind it; part military, part monastic, the ruins crown the cliffs in their isolation. Here is a site that is only to be paralleled at Whitby, a sacred site on the long Northumberland coast that ranks second only to Lindisfarne.

The history of the castle is of course intimately linked with that of the monastery, which stood on the extremity of the cliff. Its position is impregnable; three of its sides are protected by the North Sea, and the fourth, taking in the nature of the terrain, allows for an easy defence. The Romans had a fort here and the Danes used it as a military base. Prior to the Conquest it was in the possession of the Earls of Northumberland and held by an Earl Tostig. Later, William the Conqueror was to grant it, with considerable lands, to Robert de Mowbray. This powerful Earl was to defy William II and he withstood a siege of two months in the castle before it fell and he escaped to Bamburgh Castle; eventually he was caught and spent the rest of his life in prison. It was in 1296 that Edward I gave the priory a licence to crenellate the precinct walls. In 1346 when Sir William Douglas invaded England, he sent word to Prior Thomas de la Mare requesting that dinner should not take place until he arrived. He came, but not as the victor he expected, but defeated with King David at Neville's Cross; Douglas came as a prisoner. Like Dunstanburgh the gatehouse also served as the keep; and a barbican similar to that at Alnwick defended it. It dates from the time of Prior John de Wethamstede and was completed in 1390 with the help of Richard II and John of Gaunt. The entrance is a tunnel-vaulted archway with guard-chambers followed by a stretch that was open to the sky but flanked by high walls. This crosses the ditch where there was a drawbridge. Then follows the gatehouse proper; again we have a tunnel-vaulted archway with another open stretch, before we reach a third gateway that completes the layout. On the first floor of the gatehouse is the Great Hall with its tall transomed windows and large fireplace. Adjoining it, though not as high, is the kitchen with its wide fireplace and huge oven. Above the hall is the solar of the gatehouse, which also has transomed windows. The main staircase leading to the upper floors is in the north-east corner of the kitchen. At the north-west corner of the curtain wall we have what is left of the Whitely Tower, a remnant of the fourteenth century; the walls to the north and east have fallen into the sea. In 1539, when the priory was dissolved, Sir John Lee reported that it was 'a place so needful to be fortified as none within the realm more'. In 1545 a thousand men were employed and £2,633-4s-3d was spent; this was mostly on wages since the stone was close at hand. But within fifty years the castle was again found to be in need of repair when its Captain Sir John Fenwick reported that it had become uninhabitable.

This promontory has witnessed a great deal: the Vikings followed by the Romans; it is the burial site of two Northumbrian kings: Oswin of Deira and Osred; and not far away set on a 50-foot column is the statue of Admiral Collingwood. For well over 1,300 years monastic buildings of some sort have stood here. Today it is in the capable hands of English Heritage.

WARKWORTH CASTLE

The cross-shaped keep of Warkworth stands like a sentinel on the neck of a peninsular formed by the River Coquet; Shakespeare immortalised it by setting Act II, Scene 3, of *Henry IV Part 2* here. The earliest known record of Warkworth is in 737 when Ceolwulf, King of Northumbria, gave it to the monks of Lindisfarne. First built in the twelfth century as a motte and bailey castle, every century since has left a mark upon it, and the great ruin that greets today's visitor is one of the most impressive examples of a fortified residence. In 1158 Henry II gave the castle and manor to Roger Fitz Richard for bravery in battle. His family were to hold it for almost 200 years before Edward III gave it to Henry de Percy, head of one of England's most powerful medieval families in 1332. This was in part payment of expenses incurred defending the North against the Scots. The Percies at once began to improve its defences, and replaced the previous building with a three-storey keep of unique shape, a cross superimposed on a square. While the lower levels housed guards and servants, the earls' quarters were above. The most famous of the Percies who were connected with Warkworth were the 1st Earl of Northumberland and his son, Harry 'Hotspur', whose name is enshrined in the ballad as the reckless hero of the battles of Otterburn and Homildon Hill. It was here that the Earl took part in the conspiracy against Henry IV; it was their support that had placed him on the throne in 1399. It ended with the death of his son Henry 'Hotspur' at Shrewsbury in 1403 and his own exile. The estates were forfeited, and then restored by royal clemency to 'Hotspur''s son, who was to become the 2nd Earl and Warden of the Eastern Marches; he was to show his devotion to the king by giving his life during the Wars of the Roses. In 1569 the Percy estates were once again confiscated when they took part in the ill-fated 'Rising of the North'. When news of revolt reached the ears of Queen Elizabeth I she was incensed:

> The newes unto London came in all the speede that
> ever might be, and word is brought to our Royall
> Queene of the rising in the north countrie. Her
> Grace she turned round about, and like a Royall
> Queene she swore, I will ordayne them such a
> breakfast as never was seen in the north before.

Subsequently Sir John Forster, the Warden of the Middle Marches, plundered the castle to such an extent that when James I came to Warkworth in 1617 he looked at the Percy Lion on the keep and

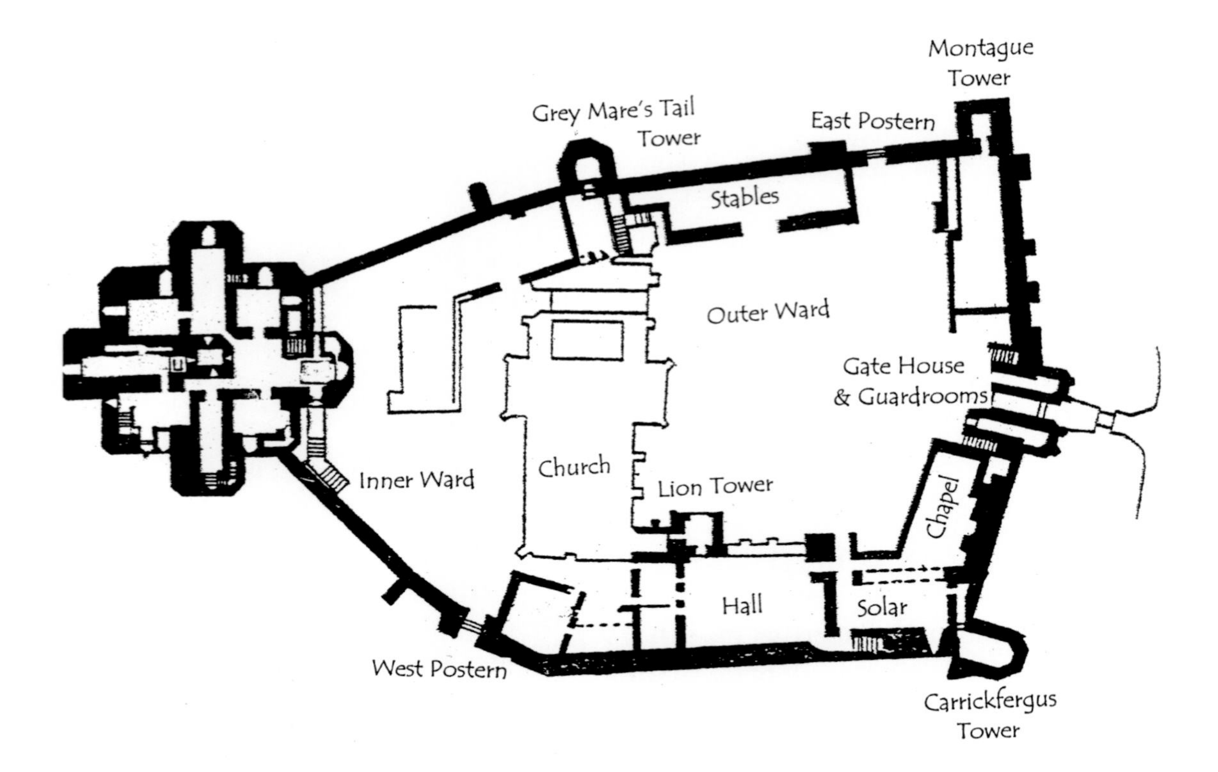

said, 'this lyone houldes up this castle'; and his advisors were 'much moved to see it soe spoyled and soe badly kept'. In 1672 more damage was done when the Earl's widow allowed John Clarke take away 272 wagonloads of lead, timber and other materials; he is said to have used this to build his manor house at Chirton.

Although there is no evidence of it the castle closely follows the lines of a motte and bailey castle; the keep stands on the motte some 75 feet from the gatehouse. The gatehouse is a good example of Early English architecture. In front of it is a moat, which would have been crossed by a drawbridge; its recesses are still to be seen. Like those at Alnwick and Bothal, the gatehouse displays two semi-octagonal turrets at the angle towards the field; but they differ from these in several aspects, the two south corners are strengthened to two thirds of their height; the doorways to the guard chambers are not placed in the sides of the vaulted passage, as usual, but round the corner; finally, access to the floor above was gained by a stair on either side the passage. To the left of the gatehouse are the ruins of a chapel, and beyond this against the curtain wall, the remains of the Great Hall and solar. The Lion Tower was built as the main porch to the Great Hall; over the doorway is the Percy Lion that gives the tower its name. This large and portentous beast, with its crescent collar, is sculptured on a panel that occupies most of the east face of the tower. Within the outer bailey were a series of buildings. On the west side were the domestic quarters, while on the east were the offices, stores and stables. The Carrickfergus Tower at the south-east corner has loop-holes at its base; this was possibly intended for a group of crossbowmen. Effectively separating the inner bailey from the outer are the remains of a building that was begun but never completed; this is the cruciform collegiate church. On the east curtain wall stands the Grey Mare Tail Tower that antiquarian Cadwaller Bates eulogized on in the nineteenth century,

> as a most remarkable perfect specimen of early-thirteenth-century military architecture. Its five external faces are each pierced by a giant cross loop 16 feet in length. These five loops, extending through the two lower stories of the tower to within a short distance of the ground, are probably the finest examples in Europe of the defensive openings adapted for the crossbow, which became peculiarly common in the thirteenth century.

The finest part of the castle is the keep; described in the survey by Bellysys, in the time of Henry VIII, 'as a marvellous proper dongeoun of viii towyres all joined in one howse together'. Pevsner tells us 'Here is one of the rare cases where military engineering happened to be a great architect'. The entrance to this complicated keep is by a flight of steps mounting the side of the motte on which it stands; and the arrangement of the various apartments must have required a great deal of thought. The plan is unusual and perhaps best described as a square with chamfered corners, superimposed on a Greek cross with chamfered edges. One of the unique features of the building is its central 'lantern' that gives light to most of the rooms and to collect the rainwater for an advanced system of flushing the various garderobes. On the ground floor, are the guardrooms and cellars which are entirely vaulted, and four staircases; the vestibule at the entrance has a hidden pit below the floor that was a trap for the Scots. A narrow passage from the Great Hall leads to two rooms that have fine sea views; and a newel stair in the corner gives access to two similar suits. The second floor contains the private apartments of the Duke of Northumberland and is not open to the public.

Today Warkworth Castle remains embalmed in the past, a place of shattered walls and dark corridors; its massive keep and high turrets has altered little since the fifteenth century. The castle does have one of the vital essentials of all mediaeval romances, which in spite of their frequency in stories are in fact quite rare – an underground dungeon.

Unlikely as it may seem today, it was only by chance that Warkworth did not become the seat of the Duke's of Northumberland; it was at a time when the estate came into the possession of the Duke of Somerset through his marriage with the heiress of the last Earl of Northumberland; he dithered over restoring Warkworth or Alnwick, before settling on the latter. Fortunately in choosing Alnwick the Duke ensured that Warkworth escaped restoration; still roofed the keep remains an unspoilt example of medieval architecture of the day.

WARKWORTH BRIDGE TOWER

The tower at Warkworth Bridge is a rare late-fourteenth-century stone gatehouse, built to fortify the bridge. The central bridge support is hexagonal in shape, having two ribbed arches either side of it, and is now the only remaining fortified medieval bridge in England; the gatehouse stands at the south end. Up until 1830 a cross with the Percy coat of arms stood on the bridge. A passage runs through the square lower storey of the gatehouse and on to the bridge, but sadly the upper storey machicolations have now become ruinous. During the nineteenth century this fine gate tower was, for a short period of time, the local gaol. The bridge is a Scheduled Monument and a Grade II listed building.

WHITTON TOWER, ROTHBURY

Standing on the south side of the Coquet, half a mile from the town, is the fortified rectory of Rothbury. It was built in the fourteenth century by the Umfravilles as part of the line of peles that extended from Hepple to Warkworth. The tower, one of the best preserved in the county, dates, along with others, from the earliest of times, being mentioned with Carrington and Hepple in the survey of 1415. Because of the surrounding trees the tower is best seen from the garden. It is unique in having vaulted rooms on both the first and second floors. The reason for this is due to the slope of the ground: its height changes from 40 feet on the south side to 60 feet on the north. From the ground floor a newal stair leads to the summit of the tower. The builder was to use this slope to get an ample supply of water. In the lowest part of the building is the cellar, once used as a byre, in which the rectors secured their cattle from the marauding reivers. There is also a well some 3 feet in diameter and 9 feet deep. During alterations in the nineteenth century, a recess was to reveal what must have been the private chapel of the rectors before the Reformation. Whitton is one of the eight Northumbrian towers that have a carved shield built into the west front. Enough remains of this weather-worn shield to show a coat of arms to be cinquefoil within an orle of six crosses Moline, a coat which closely resembles that of the Umfraville arms.

In 1679 the Rev. John Thomlinson wrote:

> At my coming to Rothbury, the parsonage house
> besides its darkness and smokiness, not to be endured
> had, (for want of covering to keep it dry), all the
> wood of it perfectly rotten, the floors as well as
> that which belonged to the roof and to say nothing
> of the stable etc. actually lying in their ruins.

This is now a Grade II* listed building protected by law.

WOODHOUSE BASTLE, HEPPLE

No one has portrayed the reivers more clearly than Bishop Leslie. 'When being taken,' he wrote 'they have so much persuasive eloquence, and so many smooth and insinuating words at command, that if they do not move their judges, nay and even their adversaries, to have mercy, yet they incite them to admiration and compassion.'

Located on high ground, just off the Grasslees to Holystone Road, stands the bastle of Woodhouses. Built in the sixteenth century, and unique to the Border region, the Bastle house was built by the wealthier farmer to protect their families and livestock from reivers. Woodhouses is an impressive instance of one of these houses. The vaulted ground floor with its stone staircase is a typical feature of these fortified dwellings. In 1602 William Potte, the farmer here, had his initials and date carved in the stone above the door. When the house was attacked by reivers stock would be barred in at the ground floor. The family, occupying the upper floor, used the stone spout above the doorway to pour hot liquids on to enemies. James Allan the great Northumbrian Piper was born here; in 1810, he was condemned to death for horse stealing. This sentence was to be later commuted to one of life imprisonment.

In 1597 Richard Fenwick was to remark: 'If Jesus Christ were emongest them, they would deceave him.'

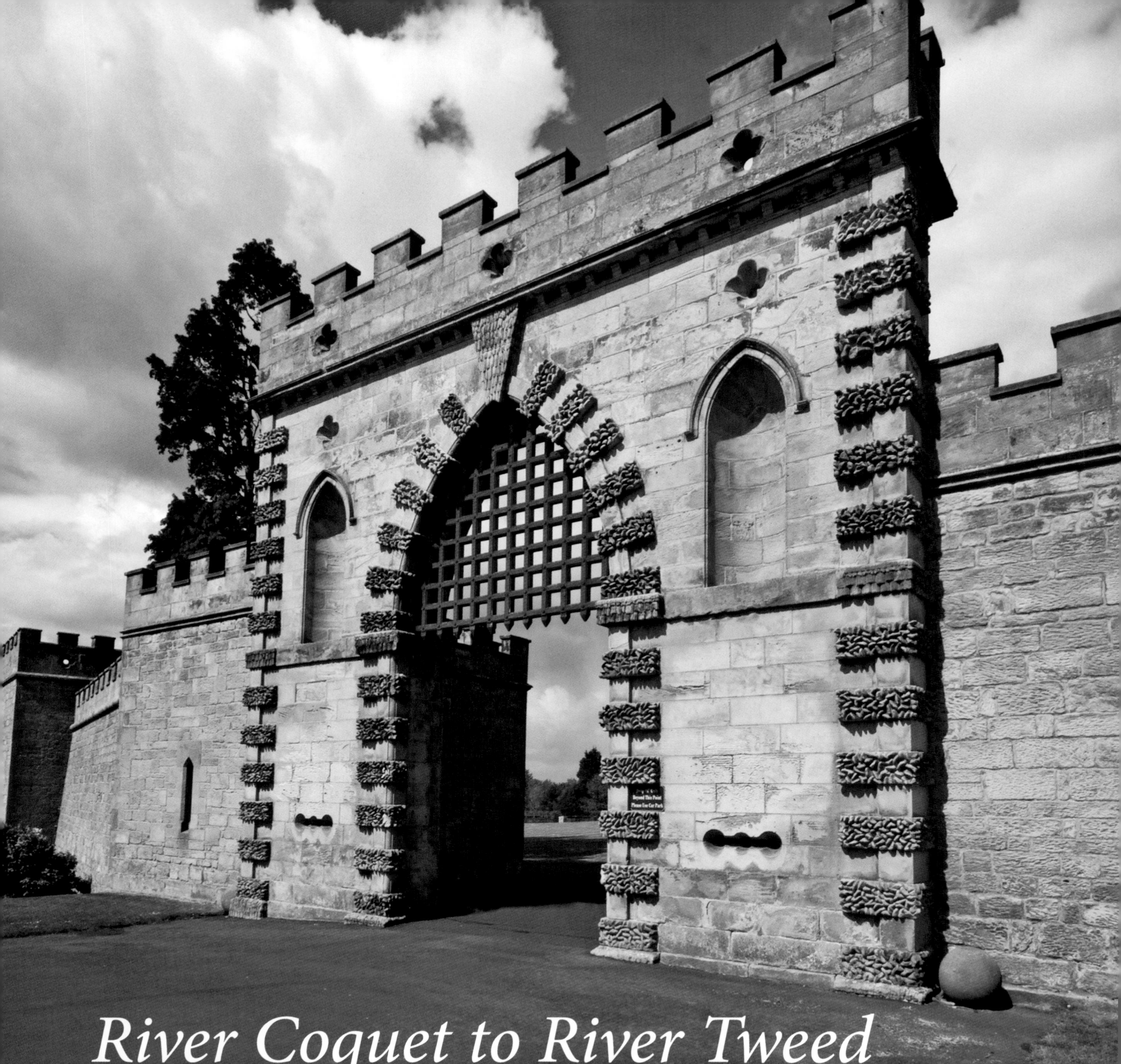

River Coquet to River Tweed

ALNHAM TOWER

Alnham lies at the foot of the Cheviots, and as its name implies is in the valley of the Aln. Its siting, on the edge of the hills, was very precarious in former days and one is not surprised to learn that it was an object of repeated attacks. Known locally as 'Yeldom' it is easily reached from Alwinton, Whittingham or Rothbury. The present pele, built in the late-fourteenth century, is first mentioned in the Border survey of 1541: 'At Alname be two leytle toures whereof thone ys the mansion of the vycaredge'. This stone tower lies just to the west of the church. Like most houses of its kind the ground floor has a vaulted basement, which may have been a storage area. There is no obvious access between the ground floor and the first floor; access to the upper storey was probably by means of an external ladder.

Today the old tower forms a picturesque part of the house; its battlements are finished in a similar manner to those at Whittingham Tower.

ALNWICK CASTLE

Described by the Victorians as 'Windsor of the North', Alnwick Castle is the second largest of the inhabited castles in England; it is a masterpiece of medieval grandeur. It was the Norman Ivo de Vescis who first was granted the land on which Alnwick stood, and unlikely as it may seem there was a time when the castle was in such a poor state of repair that it was almost abandoned by the Dukes of Northumberland in favour of Warkworth as their seat. The castle dates from the eleventh century, when Eustace-fitz-John married Beatrix de Vesci the then heiress of Alnwick. Its history is steeped in the Border wars when Northumberland was almost as often in Scottish hands as those of the English with only the Debatable Lands between the two countries, and whose boundaries from one year to the next were rarely the same. It was in 1309 that a new era in the history of the castle began with its purchase by Henry de Percy; the word purchase, however, hardly fits the shady

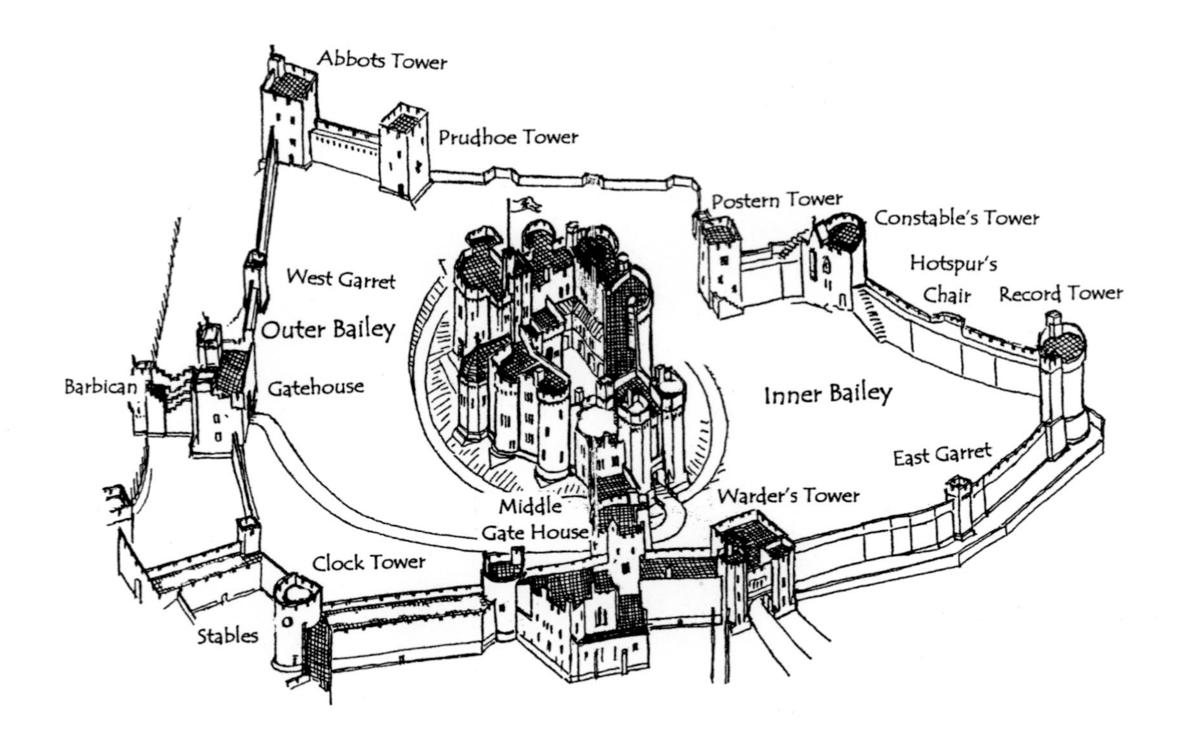

deal which took place. The estate at the time had been left in the trust of Bishop Bek, the authoritive Prince Bishop; deliberately picking a quarrel with the son and heir of William de Vesci, he made allegations that gave the excuse to sell the estate and castle and keep the money. Alnwick Castle came into the possession of Henry Percy when it was at a critical period of its history. Within a few years Bannockburn was to be fought and lost by Edward II, and Northumberland was overrun by Scots to avenge the humiliation inflicted on them. Following the death of Harry 'Hotspur''s father the estates then became forfeit to the crown until they were restore by Henry V, who secured the Percies allegiance once more to the house of Lancaster. The 6th Earl became betrothed to Anne Boleyn. Unfortunately for him Henry VIII then became her admirer and their engagement was broken off, and in the Gunpowder Plot of 1605 Thomas Percy became embroiled in the plot and was committed to the Tower. With the death of the 11th Earl in 1750 the line of succession died out and the vast Percy estates through various marriages were divided and passed to a Yorkshire Baronet, Sir Hugh Smithson. In 1766 he was created Duke of Northumberland and Earl Percy.

The visitor to the castle enters it from Bailifgate. The main entrance is a strong barbican, built across the old castle ditch, which was crossed by a drawbridge from the gatehouse. In the past the barbican was guarded by a moat, with water supplied from the Bow Burn, and attackers who cleared it were then exposed to assault from above. Tar, molten lead and arrows were showered down from the tower ahead, while on the battlements warlike stone figures of soldiers mingled with the living to defend the walls. On the curtain wall to the immediate left of the gatehouse is the small stone tower of the West Garret, and in the corner the Abbot's Tower built by the first Percy, where the Abbot of Alnwick Abbey used to lodge whenever his presence was required at the castle. From there the wall turns at right angles to the east and terminates at the rebuilt Falconer's Tower. To the right of the gatehouse is the Clock Tower, which leads through to the stables. Then follows the Auditor's Tower. We are told that this tower is so called because the 6th Earl imprisoned a man called William Worme, one of his auditors, here 'until he has accounted for more money received than ever I received'. Passing through the Middle gatehouse we now come into the inner bailey, on the left, the entrance to the inner courtyard of the keep. To the left of it is the Postern Tower and adjoining Constable's Tower. A sentry walk to the right leads us past Hotspur's Chair to the Record Tower. From here along another short stretch of sentry walk we pass the East Garret to the Warden's Tower. The entrance to the keep, flanked by two octagonal towers, is through a finely groined and

arcaded portico from the inner bailey. The inner courtyard has a triple arched well with a keel-moulded surround.

In the nineteenth century Algernon, the 4th Duke, decided to refurbish the keep in the Renaissance style using Salvin as architect. For this he employed over 300 artists and workmen to complete the work. The result is the richly decorated interior we see today since only minor alterations have taken place since the restoration was complete; the principal apartments now contain a magnificent collection of paintings by Canaletto, Titian and Van Dyke.

In 1569 the household was made up of 166 men, women and children, this number excluded the high-ranking officials. Provision had to be made on a daily basis for fifty-seven visitors who might be expected to be received at the castle. The cost for feeding this huge retinue was £3-11s-6d per year. Moving from one castle to another was a major operation; as well the food that was required, 40 gallons of beer and 4 gallons of wine were consumed daily.

The garden, which is entirely enclosed by walls, is now considered to be one of the most contemporary gardens of the last century. Its patron HRH The Prince of Wales officially opened it in October 2002 when the first phase of development was complete. On entering the visitor is confronted with the spectacular Grand Cascade where over 7,000 gallons of water a minute fall over a series of weirs before disappearing beneath a walkway of four large bell-mouthed openings, to reappear once more on the other side in the form of four mounds of water. The sequence of the water displays is changed every half-hour; with four sequences over two hours. Above the grand cascade lies the small walled garden known as the Ornamental Garden. Its entrance is accessed through the wrought–iron gates set within three stone arches. Here you will find over 16,000 plants with their plantings designed so that they flower at different times of the year. Standing on the edge of the Rose Garden, at the base of the cascade, is the eighteenth-century Fox Urn. Bought with the winnings from a horse race by the 4th Duke it shows a fox sitting on top of a fruit filled vessel supported by monkeys; it is decorated with the figures of cherubs and masks that depict the four seasons. The 4th Duke was also responsible for bringing the Venetian wrought-iron gates that hang at the entrance to the Ornamental Garden from Italy. An array of more than 3,000 roses can be found in the pergola-lined walkways of the Rose Garden; these have been donated by many of the top rose growers in the country. At the Chelsea Flower Show of 2001, and to coincide with the creation of the Alnwick Garden, David Austin launched a new English rose. Known as the Alnwick

Castle Rose, it blossoms from early summer to the first frost. The locked wrought-iron gates that protect the Poison Garden remind one of the dangers that grow within; and once the visitor has emerged from the ivy-covered tunnels they will see before them the plants in flame-shaped beds. Some of them have to be kept behind bars for safety. Sited high in the trees outside the walls of the garden is the Treehouse; it is one of the largest of its kind in the world. This beautifully crafted treetop house features a variety of suspended walkways and rope bridges.

The garden, an all-weather attraction, is now in its second phase of development.

ANCROFT TOWER

In a district so restless and unsafe for many centuries, the motto 'any port in a storm' springs to mind; in some cases the port took the form of a church tower. It was not often, however, that a pele was built on to the end of the church, but this is what happened at Ancroft, a hamlet 5 miles from the border. The church that the monks of Lindisfarne built in the thirteenth century for this thriving hamlet had only a chancel and nave; but in the fourteenth century a tower, more military in character than ecclesiastical, was attached. Built into the nave of the church for the protection of the parson and his flock, it blocked the twelfth century doorway. Entry to the tower was then only via the church, with a spiral stair giving access to the upper floors. The bellcote on the roof contains two bells, one of which was taken from John Wesley's chapel in London. In the years when plague swept Ancroft infected people were taken to a nearby field known as Broomie's Huts and a bower of broom was placed over them; when they died, their bodies were burned with the broom.

BAMBURGH CASTLE

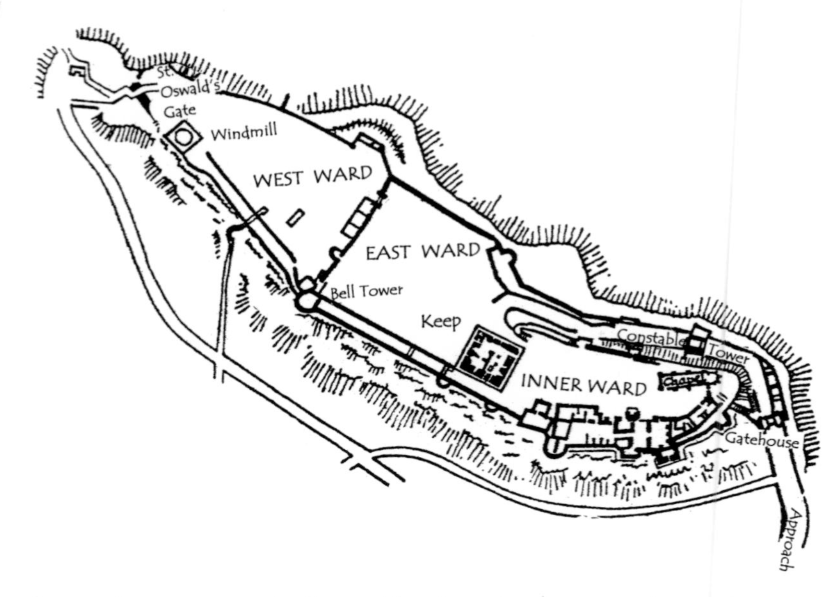

Bamburgh was not only the centre of the kingdom but also the centre of the Christian faith in a land that was in the main still pagan. The castle, crouched on a basalt crag within sight of Holy Island, is, without doubt, one of the most striking sites in Northumberland; it is an impregnable fortress. Medieval in appearance, it rises in brooding grandeur to dominate both the village and coast; only the empty sand dunes and cold North Sea lie beyond. It was in AD 547 that the capital of Northumbria got its present name, given by King Ethelfrith to his wife Bebba – Bebbanburgh became Bamburgh. Ethelfrith was grandson of King Ida 'the flamebearer'. Bede tells us in *Historia Brittonum* that

> The brave and ambitious king, Ethelfrith governed the kingdom of the Northumbrians, and ravaged the Britons more than all the chiefs of the English, insomuch that he might be compared to Saul of old, king of the Israelites, save only in this, that he was ignorant of Divine religion. For he conquered more territories from the Britons than any other chieftain or king, either subduing the inhabitants and making them a tributary, or driving them out and planting the English in their places.

In the year AD 651 Penda, king of the Mercians, attacked Bamburgh and, being unable to take it by either assault or siege, he was determined to destroy it by fire. Bishop Aidan of Lindisfarne, who was in retreat on the Farne Islands at the time, saw from a distance the threat to the northern capital. 'See Lord, what ill Penda does!' he cried. As if in answer to his prayer the wind then changed direction and drove the smoke and flames into the attackers faces. William Rufus besieged it in 1095 during the rebellion led by Robert de Mowbray. The Earl escaped to Tynemouth while his wife held the fort until his capture; it was only when the King threatened to put out his eyes that she surrendered: a full account of the story is to be seen in the *Anglo-Saxon Chronicles*. In 1164 a new keep was built which was completed by 1170, at a cost, it is recorded, of £4.

Throughout the middle ages the history of the castle is not of great interest; it was only one of the many Border fortresses.

The castle, maintained by Edward I, was to be neglected by Edward II, and with the decline of the kingdom the castle slowly fell into decay; by the time of Edward III it was reported that such was the state of disrepair that it would soon become ruinous. A few years later it had undergone sufficient repairs for Edward III to leave Philippa his Queen here, while he went on to besiege Berwick.

The bulk of Bamburgh Castle is huge, almost 8 acres, and stretches to almost a quarter of a mile in length. It consists of three wards or baileys that occupy between them the whole top of the basalt rock. The approach is from the south-east by a twisting road that leads up to the barbican. Two flanking towers guard the outer gate; beyond is a passage that cuts through the rock and leads to the Inner Bailey. To the west of this are two other wards, called the East Ward and the West Ward, but these are little more than enclosures. The East Ward is separated from the West Ward by a curtain wall, at the south end of which is the Clock Tower. Archaeologists have discovered material here dating back twelve centuries. The keep lies at the edge of the Inner Bailey. There is a second entrance to the East Bailey and, within this area, are the remains of a twelfth-century chapel; it has a nave, chancel and apse. The chancel is said to be on the actual site of the Saxon church where Saint Aidan died on 31 August 651. The early Norman keep at Bamburgh dominates the site. Its walls built of red sandstone are 9–10 feet thick. The unusually small stone with which it was built came from the quarries at North Sunderland; this was to make easy the portage by men on horseback. A nail-studded door at ground level beneath a decorated Norman arch forms the entrance to the keep. In the vaulted basement is a well cut 150 feet through the basalt and sandstone, Simeon of Durham tells us that in the twelfth-century, 'there is in the western side, and in the highest part of the city, a fountain hollowed out in a marvellous fashion, and the water of which is sweet to drink and most limpid to the sight'. Legend tells us of the jealous queen who changed her stepdaughter into the loathly Laidley Worm, said to reside at the bottom of this well in the shape of a toad. The toad is said to crawl out of the well every seven years, seeking revenge on innocent maidens. There are also two huge chains, known as 'King Ida's watch chains'; these were once used for raising sunken ships.

By Tudor times Bamburgh was reported once more to be in a ruinous state. Early in the eighteenth century the castle came into the possession of Nathaniel Liewe, Bishop of Durham, one of the richest and most powerful churchmen of the time. On his death he left the castle as part of a charitable trust; when Walter White visited Bamburgh he found there 'a school, a dispensary, a store for the sale of grain and groceries at a low price for the poor, and a system for the prevention and relief of shipwreck'.

In 1894 the castle was bought by the Victorian inventor Lord Armstrong, who restored it in the Gothic manner. It now houses the Armstrong Museum with its fine collections.

From the top of the keep, or encircling ramparts the views are magnificent; and it is not difficult to let one's mind drift back through time to some of the more stirring events of the past. Sacked by the Danes in 993 it remained desolate until the time of the Norman Conquest. William Rufus set up a wooden structure called a malvoisin when the Earl of Northumberland was besieged here; and later the Earl's young bride, Countess Matilda, was faced with the choice of surrendering the castle or seeing her husband's eyes put out. Edward II came ashore here from a small boat beneath the walls after his defeat at Bannockburn. After a fortnight's siege in 1462, and when the garrison had eaten all of their horses, it surrendered to the Earl of Warwick on Christmas Eve. Two years later, the bombardment by the King's great guns was to cost Bamburgh dearly: for every shot fired a head was taken.

BARMOOR CASTLE, LOWICK

The Muschampe family built a 'holde' or tower at Barmoor when the manor, as well as the Barony of Wooler, was bestowed on them in the reign of Henry I. But although it played host to both Edward I and Edward II, it was not until the reign of Edward III that a licence to crenellate the tower was given on 17 May 1341. It is interesting to note at this time that the Muschampes were still paying a tithe to the shrine of St Cuthbert to ensure burial within the walls of the Island Priory; the tithe was made up of a house and croft, 4 acres of arable land, the village field and 100 loads of peat. The English army were to camp here at Lowick the day after the Battle of Flodden in 1513, and it was here that Henry V and the Wardens of the Marches gathered with an army of 100,000 men in retribution for a Scots attack on the English near the border in 1417.

Slowly the Border warfare began to take its toll on Barmoor until finally, in 1541, the building was counted among those fortresses which were destroyed by the Scots; in a report lodged at Newcastle it was described as 'ruinous and in extreme decay due to lack of repair'. By 1548 the castle could only parade seven men. The turbulent years that were to follow had drastic results on the Muschampe fortunes; so it was, that, on 23 February 1649, Lady Muschampe formally gave up administration of the castle in favour of her husband's creditors. In 1661 the London office of Watts and Blackborrow were to gain possession of Barmoor and they in turn conveyed it to one William Carr Esq. of Gray's Inn. Over the years it was to pass though a variety of hands until it came into the possession of Francis Sitwell; he was to oversee in its transformation. The design of the house was by the architect John Patterson of Edinburgh. Patterson, who had trained under Adams, was to produce designs in the 'castle style of Adams', which introduced a new era of elegance at Barmoor. The entrance hall and principal rooms are of oval shape and the fittings are in the Adams style. Over the stairs is an oval glass dome. Incorporated into the building are the old walls of the tower house and a Jacobean porch. The banqueting suite was the garden side. It is still castellated and has round corner towers.

According to legend it is here on Lowick Moor that the 'Ladye of Barmoor' transforms herself into an amazing white hare; she was reputed to have dealings with fairies. The story forms the theme of a ballad in Sheldon's *Minstrelsy of the English Borders.*

BEADNELL TOWER

Sheltering behind the sand dunes in the small village of Beadnell is an inn which was once a pele tower. The building, now known as The Craster Arms, lies at the centre of the village and contains the remains of a medieval tower house that form the rear half of the main building. The outside of the building is embellished with the Craster coat of arms: a raven and the inspiring motto 'Dum vivo spero' (While there's life there's hope). The raven or crow is a pun on the family name, which was formerly spelled Crawster. The basement, divided in two by a cross wall is vaulted, and a newal staircase once went from here to the first floor. The earliest reference to it is in the will of Thomas Forster in 1587, when he left it to his son.

The name Beadnell is thought to come from the word 'Bedewine'.

BERWICK CASTLE AND ELIZABETHAN RAMPARTS

The compact town of Berwick, on the north bank of the Tweed, had changed hands thirteen times before it was to finally become English in 1482. Geographically speaking Berwick is neither in England or Scotland; England extends north of the Tweed, yet the Tweed is a Scottish river; Berwick is a Scottish Burgh, yet Northumberland does the policing. It has the misfortune of being of dual nationality. Its name, Bere or Bar Wic, meaning corn or grain, is most probably of Saxon origin. It was a Scottish burgh and port with a great deal of trade. Some idea of its prosperity may be taken from the fact that in 1287 its Customs & Excise collected about £2,000; this was at a time when those of the whole of England produced little more than £8,000. But it is of its tribulations, rather than of its prosperity that one thinks, such as the time when Edward I, in 1296, inflicted a terrible vengeance on the rebellious John Balliol, massacring 7,000 of Berwick's inhabitants without distinction of age or sex. Thirty Flemish merchants would be burnt alive whilst defending themselves in the Red Hall. As for the callous treatment meted out to the Countess of Buchan, who had recklessly and on her own authority crowned Bruce at Scone, she was shut in a cage for four years and hung out over the castle wall 'for all to see who passed that way'.

The first record of the town is in a charter of Edgar, King of Scotland, when he conferred Berwick and all its possessions on the see of Durham. Since then it has had a troubled history; for over 300 years it was the cockpit of England and Scotland. One day it would belong to Scotland, and on the next to England, and a few hundred people would die during the transfer. It has seen more fighting than any other town in Great Britain; and with the exception of Jerusalem, of any town in the world. Little wonder that today, there is only the shattered walls of what was one of the most famous of castles on the border. In 1147 William the Lion of Scotland stood in chains at Berwick before Henry II and surrendered the town as being a part of his ransom; later, Richard I was to cede it back to the Scots in return for money for his Crusade. Wallace was to capture the town in 1297 but it was soon relieved, and after his execution one of his limbs was set up on a pole at Berwick Bridge. After his victory at Homildon Hill in 1333 Edward

III regained the town but it was lost again while he was busy in France. It was recovered, but lost once more by Richard II and then retaken. Throughout the fourteenth and fifteenth centuries Berwick was, at various times, to suffer at the hands of besiegers. It wasn't until the Wars of the Roses, when it was surrendered by Henry VI and then regained by Richard Duke of York, that it became English for the last time. With the Union of the two countries the castle was allowed to fall into decay and the stones from it used for the new town walls. Of the castle today only two or three towers stand, but at the south-west is a line of curtain wall called the White Wall; flanked by the 'Breakneck Steps', it descends the steep slopes to the river. The construction of the railway in 1847 was to complete its destruction, and the Great Hall where Edward I once presided over a distinguished assembly to choose a Scottish king is now the down platform.

The circuit of Berwick walls is something that no one with an opportunity should miss. Work began on building the walls as soon as Edward I had captured the town in 1296. At first this was just a palisade, but it was soon replaced by stone. The broad promenade on the summit of the ramparts lifts one up above the town and has the adjacent sea lying to the east. For some time the walls of Berwick had been difficult to keep in a state of good repair and in the face of the ever-present danger from Scotland Elizabeth I decided to shorten the perimeter walls. This was done at great expense and in the most up-to-date military style. The work is based on the lines of the contemporary walls at Lucca and Verona and was designed by two Italian engineers, Contio and Portinari, their objective being to make best use of the flanking fire of their artillery. The walls are now the best surviving example of their kind in Europe.

On a lighter note the name of Tweed will always be associated with salmon, and on the south bank of the river the old custom of crowning the Salmon Queen was revived after a long absence, and the old custom of 'Riding the Bounds' is still carried out on 1 May. And for those who don't know, Northumberland ends near to the 'Steps of Grace', which were immortalised by John Buchan in his book *The Thirty-nine Steps* and not, as many travellers believe, at the Royal Border Bridge.

CALLALY CASTLE

Close to Whittingham and in one of the most secluded parts of the Vale of Aln, Callaly Castle encloses the ancient tower of the Claverings, where they lived for almost 500 years. The family came here after the de Callaleys who held the estate by a tenure that included sending a cart to Bamburgh with the trunk of a tree for the King's hearth on alternate days between Whitsuntide and Lammas. The Claverings, who acquired the property in the latter part of the thirteenth century, had some distinguished descendants: a King of England, a Queen of England, a Duchess of York, an Earl of Westmoreland, an Earl of Northumberland, the Earl of Warwick and an Earl Marshal of England. Robert Clavering died in 1582 during the reign of Elizabeth I and his will makes interesting reading. Included in the inventory of his goods are: one black cloak faced with taffeta valued at 40 shillings; a long furred gown at 46s-8d; a stone and a half of English iron at 16d a stone, two firkins of soap and five swerms of bees in the garden.

Included in the list of Border fortresses in 1415, Callaly does not even slightly resemble a castle; it is in fact a pele tower. The medieval tower now forms part of the west wing of the present mansion in a beautiful setting, a mixture of styles passed down through the ages. Italian stucco artists from Wallington Hall carried out the plasterwork for the showpiece drawing room to the design of James Paine.

CARTINGTON CASTLE, NEAR ROTHBURY

Cartington Castle stands on the edge of the moors, high up on the slopes to the north of the Coquet on the road from Thropton to Whittingham. There are records to show that the people of Cartington paid taxes in 1296 and throughout the fourteenth century. It is first mentioned in documents of the thirteenth century when a small parcel of land was held by John le Viscount. The first recorded owner of Cartington was one Ralph Fitzmain, a king's forester; who held it in 1154. It later passed into the hands of the Cartingtons. This medieval castle was at first a walled enclosure with four corner towers, and when it was finally completed a tower house had replaced one of the turrets; this was to form the heart of the castle. The marriage of their heiress daughter passed the manor on to the Radcliffe family, and in a similar manner the marriage of their daughter passed it on to a Widdrington. On 16 November 1515, the castle was to have a royal visitor; Margaret, Queen of Scots and her month-old baby daughter stayed here when she was on her way to Morpeth. She was so ill at the time that she had to be taken to Brinkburn Priory. The survey of 1541 tells us that it was, 'a good fortresse of twoo towres and other strong storage houses of the Inherytan'ce of Sir Cuthbert Ratclyffe'. A later member of the family, one Roger Widdrington, joined forces with Charles I during the Civil War; the castle was taken and as a result he was banished, his wife was fined £400 and Cromwell ordered the castle, then worth £8,000, to be razed to the ground.

Two tall gateposts mark the entrance in the surrounding barmkin; from it four steps lead down to a sunken courtyard beneath its ruined walls. All around the tower house there are traces of what appears to be the remains of orchards and other houses. This is a Scheduled Monument and a Grade I listed building protected by law.

CHILLINGHAM CASTLE

Chillingham Castle, the ancestral home of the Earls of Tankerville and the Greys, is one of the most interesting examples of a courtyard and corner tower plan of the fourteenth century. Originally built as a small pele in 1245, the four corner towers of the castle now enclose a small courtyard. In 1255 Henry III was to stay here, as did Edward I, on his way to Scotland to battle with William Wallace in 1298. It was not until the reign of Edward III, in 1344, that licence to crenellate was given to Thomas de Heton and his fortress here at Chillingham became a castle. A moat gave it added protection. The work must have been complete by 1348, as it was in this year that Sir Thomas Heton allowed the vicar to lodge in a room above the castle gate, and built stabling for two horses in the west hall. The survey of 1415 showed it as still belonging to the Heton family; by this time it was the Greys who owned it. As one of the most important families in the north they played a major role in keeping the marauding Scots at bay. It fell to the Scottish soldiers of James IV in 1513, but was back in the hands of the Grey's two days later when the Scots were defeated at Flodden Field. Some twenty years later, in 1536, the Percy's brought their artillery to bear on Chillingham when the Grey's refused to join in the 'Pilgrimage of Grace'. Damage to the north-west wall meant that substantial rebuilding then had to be done.

After a fire in 1803, Charles, the 5th Earl of Tankerville, called in Sir Jeffery Wyatville, architect to George IV. Fresh from his success at Windsor Castle, he laid out an Italian garden, with box hedges and limes, on the site of the medieval jousting ground. By the 1930s the once-proud castle had fallen into ruin and it was only when Sir Humphrey Wakefield began his restoration programme in the 1980s that we began to see the castle as it is today; Sir Humphrey's wife is a member of the Grey family. The Grey family have now held this stronghold, complete with jousting course, dungeons and torture chamber, for 400 years. It is thought that Sir Walter Scott may have used it as his setting for Osbaldistone Hall in *Rob Roy*.

The castle has long been regarded as possibly the most haunted site in the country. Among its many ghosts is the one of Lady Mary Berkeley searching for her husband who ran off with her sister. Desolate and broken-hearted, she lived in the castle by herself with only her baby daughter for company. The rustle of her dress can often be heard as she sweeps along the rambling corridors searching for her errant husband. Another is the famous 'blue boy', a childish wraith that is seen in the castle's Pink Room. His heart-rending cries of fear echo through the corridors upon the stroke of midnight. In the past the cries always seemed to emanate from a spot where a passage cuts through the wall into the adjoining tower. As the cries fade away a soft halo of light would appear around the four-poster bed, and the figure of a young boy dressed in blue would approach those sleeping in the room. Even today some guests complain of a blue flash coming from the wall in the dead of night. Fragments of blue clothing and the bones of a young boy were discovered behind a wall.

CLENNELL HALL

A mile north-east of Alwinton is Clennell Hall, an old pele tower that has been modernised into a country residence. It stands just off what was termed a 'Thieves Rode' in the Middle Ages and Salters Road in the eighteenth century. Although it is not included in the 1415 list of Castles and Fortalices in the county, it was in the list of Castle Towers, along the East and Middle Marches in 1541. The survey tells us that 'At Clennell ys a lytle toure of thinherytaunce of one P'cyvall Clennell, gent, newly reparelled and brattyshed by the same P'cyvall. And also he ys in makinge of a newe barmekyn about the same as his power will extende thereunto.' There were Clennells here in the reign of Edward I, and it is to them that the manor owes its name. The tower is small, being 30 × 22 feet, with walls that are almost 7 feet thick.

Inside the house the ground floor is vaulted, and has a door at one end that leads to an ascending stair in the thickness of the wall; on the first floor stands a large seventeenth-century fireplace. Also on the first floor there is a window that has a unique feature: Bates describes it as being the most interesting bit of ancient artwork he has ever seen in Northumberland. An Elizabethan plaster frieze shows us a scene that is supposed to represent Chevy Chase. The panel of course came from elsewhere.

COUPLAND CASTLE

Coupland Castle occupies a position that seems to call for a Border tower; and a strong one at that. It stands at the edge of Glendale, and was a frequent destination for the Scottish reivers. Strangely, there does not appear to have been a castle here till after the union of the two countries; the 1541 survey of the Border towers and castles tells us that there was 'no fortress or barmekyn' at Coupland. Although known as a castle, Coupland is actually a tower house, and from the earliest of times, the Couplands, being a powerful family, figured greatly in Border affairs. Perhaps the greatest was John de Coupland. In 1346 he commanded a hundred men-at-arms at the Battle of Neville's Cross, and had the honour of capturing the Scottish king. The chronicler of the day records that the knight rushed at King David dashing the axe from his hand, the king lashed out with his gauntleted hand, removing two of John's teeth.

The entrance has a date of 1594 inscribed on one side that leads to a barrel-vaulted basement. A newel, or spiral staircase, leads to the upper floors. Through two or three changes of ownership the castle has been altered and restored, but its ghost continued to haunt the castle up to the early twentieth century. Carved on a chimneybreast, in a room known as 'the haunted chamber', are the initials of George and Mary Wallace, and the date of 1619. The tower, built in the Scottish tradition, is a good example of a tower house. This is a Grade I listed building protected by law.

CRASTER TOWER

Craster Tower stands secluded among dark and clustered trees a short distance from the village of Craster. In medieval times Craster, or Crawcestre as it was then known, was one of nine villages in the parish of Embleton; long since vanished is the old fort from which the name is derived. After the Battle of Hastings Northumbria stubbornly held out against William; and when his knight Robert de Commines and his followers were massacred in Durham, he raced north for revenge. He laid everything to waste, burning Tynedale and plundering Berwick, and leaving the country from the Humber to the Tweed such a waste that it was not worthwhile surveying for the Domesday Book. After this act of revenge only a small number of northern landowners were sanctioned to retain their properties. Among them were the Crasters. Mentioned in the 1415 list of Border strongholds, the tower has a basement vault and newal staircase. In the middle of the fourteenth century Edmund Crasestir attached a tower to the old manor house. A unique feature of the tower is that it has been in the possession of the same family since Saxon times. The Craster family have now been occupants for at least 900 years – a continuity that is now rare.

DUDDO TOWER

The ruins of Duddo Tower are the most prominent feature on crags south of the village. Its shattered ruin crowns a prominent position on the road from Berwick to Ford, about 3 miles from the border. The rocky knoll from which it gets its name commands a fine view of Border country; from the Lammermuir Hills beyond the Tweed round to the Cheviots and Flodden Hill. The tower originally was about 36 feet square protected by a barmkin and in the possession of the Claverings; later it was to pass to the Greys of Wark. In 1496 James IV of Scotland destroyed it but repairs to it meant that it was to provide protection until the late sixteenth century. Although only a fragment of the building is still standing, at one time the tower had a projecting wing on the south front containing an entrance and stair.

Drawn in the nineteenth century the ruin gives us an important record of its appearance. This is now a Scheduled Monument and Grade II listed building protected by law.

DUNSTANBURGH CASTLE

On the crest of basalt ridge that overlooks Embleton Bay stands the shattered ruins of Dunstanburgh Castle; this, along with Holy Island and Bamburgh, constitutes one of the three most romantic spots on the long line of coast that stretches from Tynemouth to Berwick. It can be approached either from Craster, which is the nearest village, or Embelton.

Built by the romantic Thomas, Earl of Lancaster and High Sheriff of England, in the reign of Edward II, it covers an area of 11 acres and is the largest castle in Northumberland. Steeped in ancient lore, he dreamed of recreating the days of King Arthur and raising a second Camelot. Sadly Dunstanburgh had been complete only a short while when his life was brought to end prematurely. It was in 1322 that his opposition to his cousin Edward was to make him a traitor when he led the barons in rebellion. He was intercepted and captured by the King's men when he reached Boroughbridge; he was to die on the block at his castle in Pontefract six days later. It took eleven strokes with an axe wielded by an

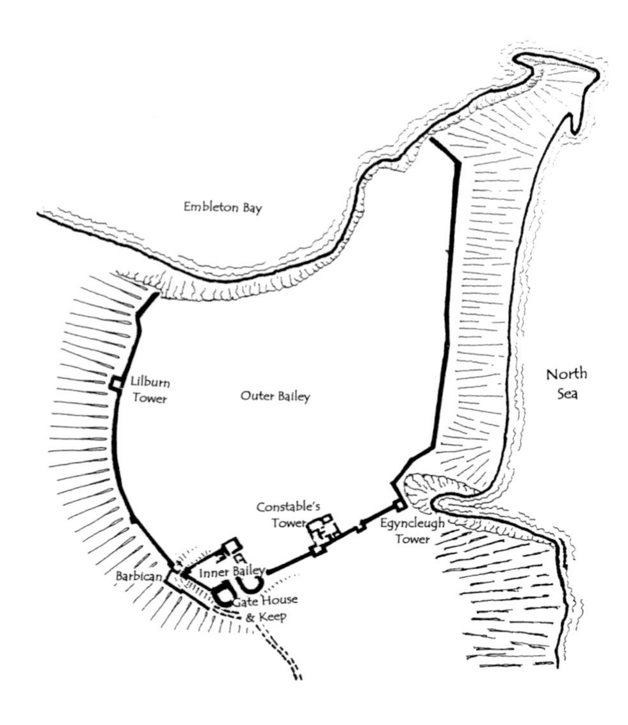

inexperienced executioner to sever his head from his body. Under the ownership of John of Gaunt, Lieutenant of the Scottish Marches, numerous alterations were made to the castle with a view to strengthen it against the Scots, then Gaunt's son seized the throne and declared himself King Henry IV; this made Dunstanburgh a royal castle. Throughout the Wars of the Roses, Dunstanburgh was a Lancastrian stronghold, changing hands a number of times. Sir Ralph Percy, known as 'the Falcon of Dunstanburgh', wavering in his allegiance to the king, first delivered the castle to the Yorkists and then to the Lancastrians; later the Earl of Warwick recaptured it. Finally, in 1524, we hear of Lord Dacre suggesting to Wolsey that lead may be taken from the castle roofs to help repair the donjon at Wark.

The 11-acre site would certainly never have been chosen were it not for the nature of land. The existing stronghold dates from about the fourteenth century. Edward II had granted it licence to crenellate in August 1316, although the work had already commenced some three years earlier. The whole of the north side is guarded by cliff; and there are no traces that a wall was ever constructed in this direction. On the west side of the castle the remains of an ashlar curtain wall curves round on top of the basalt mound. The main entrance to the castle faces to the south; approaching from Craster, we can see the great towers flanking the gateway, and a long curtain wall that stretches to the right as far as the Egyncleugh Tower. This contained the 'Water Gate' referred to in 1368. Commonly called St Margaret's Tower or Queen Margaret's Tower, it is thought to have been named after St Margaret of Scotland, although the name does not seem to have been known to the chronicler Grose, writing in 1772. Of the southern defences the gatehouse is beyond doubt magnificent. When it was in the possession of John of Gaunt the great gateway was blocked up and converted into a donjon; at the same time a new entrance was made to the north of the original doorway. This can be dated exactly, as in 1383 John of Gaunt entered into an agreement with Henry de Holme to construct a new gatehouse, to be complete with portcullis, barbican and drawbridge. The towers are square at the back, to make space on the ground floor for guardrooms; the second floor led to the Great Hall and private apartments. Within the gatehouse is the

Inner Ward; this is where the kitchen stood and also a bake house. Next to the Inner Ward is the John of Gaunt's gate, guarded by a barbican. Midway along the southern curtain wall, to the right of the gatehouse, stands the two-storey Constable's Tower. Beyond the gatehouse and northward along the curtain wall stands the Lilburn Tower; probably built by John Lilburn, the Constable here in 1323. In the huge Outer Bailey there are traces of several buildings; one circular structure is thought to be a kiln. On the eastern side there are remains of what was then the castle grange or farmstead.

By the sixteenth century the castle had fallen into decay. According to legend, a knight named Sir Guy sheltered here during a storm; on crossing the drawbridge he encountered a ghostly figure in white that bade him to enter and find a 'beauty bright'. In an ornate chamber he was surprised to find 100 knights and their horses lying asleep. In the centre of the room he saw a beautiful young maiden sleeping in a crystal casket. On either side of her were two skeletons, one holding a sword, the other a horn. The ghost told Sir Guy he could wake the young maid; but he must choose whether to use the sword or the horn to do so. Choosing the horn, he blew it; however it was the knights instead of the maid who woke. Sir Guy fainted, and when he came round the vision had gone. For the remainder of his life he was to search the ruins for the beautiful young maiden; but he was never to find her again. Now the ghost of Sir Guy the seeker continues to search the ruins in his lonely quest to find her.

EDLINGHAM CASTLE

Edlingham Castle lies below Corby's Crags, 5 miles south-west of Alnwick on the road to Rothbury. The gaunt ruins of the castle lie beside the wooded banks of Edlingham Burn. Built in the twelfth century, the castle was held by John, son of Walden, for the annual rent of a soar-hawk, or, if in default, sixpence, payable to the lord of the barony. Sir William de Felton, who added a palisade inside the moat and a gatehouse on the north side, took over the property in 1276. This was a tower house of a better kind, the basement being vaulted. The main part consists of a tall tower-house and has huge angle-buttresses corbelled at the top with small overhanging turrets. The entire keep, both outside as well as in, is built with fine ashlar. The remains of a barmkin, which held the domestic buildings, are enclosed to the north by a curtain wall. On the west side the remains of a newal stair can be seen; this went up to all floors.

By the sixteenth century, the castle had passed into the possession of the Swinburnes. An inventory of one of their wills gives us an interesting insight into what life was like in the sixteenth century. Of the bedrooms the furniture was very sparse, beds complete with feather bolsters and pillows; the kitchen equipped with 2 pots; a pan; 2 spits; a frying pan; 15 peuder platters; 13 pewter dishes; 7 saucers; 4 plates; a charger or two; a basing; a pestle and mortar; a pair of tongs; wan sylver salt parcell gilt and wan dozen of sylver spoons, the whole valued at £8. As for the deceased's clothing we have a doublet of satin overlaid with silver lace, a velvet cloak, a velvet hat and a satin gown. The most treasured of all his possessions were two horses: a white one valued at £10 and a black one at £8.

In the seventeenth century, England was still using the Julian calendar; it had not yet changed to the Gregorian calendar. It was also the time of the witch, and Northumberland at that time employed a witchfinder. By 1682, when the Swinburnes had ceased to occupy the castle, they employed an agent to live there, and one of these suffered some stressful times as a result of one known as Margaret Stothard, a witch. On one occasion, and to prevent the hair on his head from standing 'on end upward', he jumped from his bed to read his bible. Before 1978 the remains of Edlingham Castle were little more than one more ruined tower. The excavations that took place in 1978 and 1982 were to shed light on a previously unknown fortified manor house, of which only the tower remained. The newly exposed footings now show the entire plan of a small but complex manor or castle.

EDLINGHAM TOWER

In 737 Edlingham was one of the five villages that King Ceowulph gave to Holy Island Abbey. From the Alnwick road the traveller can look down and see both church and castle standing out clearly in the valley below. The Church of St John the Baptist dates back to the middle of the twelfth century. With its great walls and arrow-slit windows, the old tower is a harsh reminder of when even the church was fortified. The porch, with its round-headed doorway and barrel-vaulted roof, is one of the few Norman porches in Northumberland.

Edlingham will always be remembered as being the birthplace of the witch Margaret Stothard, who was reputed to have mystical powers. Although a mass of evidence was brought against her she escaped the fate that befell so many witches in those days. An account of the charges is recounted in Mackenzie's *History of Northumberland*.

Selected Cases of Conscience Touching Witches and Witchcraft, published in 1664, states:

> In every place and parish, every old woman with
> a wrinkled face, a furred brow, a hair lip, a gobber
> tooth, a squint eye, a squeaky voice, a scolding tongue,
> having a rugged coat on her back, a skullcap on her
> head, a spindle in her hand, a dog or cat by her side,
> is not only suspected but pronounced for a witch.

Three thousand people thought to be guilty of witchcraft are said to have been killed in England since Henry VIII.

EMBLETON VICAR'S PELE

The tower at Embleton dates from the early fourteenth century and is one of only three fortified vicarages in the county; the defensive additions to the tower date from the year 1385 when the vicar was granted licence to crenellate his residence.

Three storeys in height, it is built in a mixture of rubble and squared stone. The tower is unique in two ways; firstly, it has two vaulted rooms in the basement where other examples have only one; secondly, it is very long. It also has a very interesting feature: a secret chamber approached by a newal stair and lit only by a crack in the walls. The belfry windows are alike to those in the tower at Ponteland; which also belongs to Merton College.

ETAL CASTLE

On the banks of the River Till a row of attractive cottages makes up the picturesque village of Etal; it also boasts the thatched and whitewashed Black Bull Inn. At the end of the street is the forlorn ruin of Etal castle, built in the fourteenth century for Sir Robert de Manners.

On 3 May 1341 Sir Robert de Manners, in constant conflict with Border raids and bitter rivals, obtained a licence to crenellate his mansion house at Etal. The work is believed to have been undertaken by the masons who worked on Ford Castle three years earlier. An imposing fortress, it was partially destroyed by James IV of Scotland when he invaded England in 1496 and again in 1513; however after his demise on Flodden Field the tower was used to store the captured Scottish cannon. Although owned by the Manners family the king's forces garrisoned it; the Collingwood family were there to act as constables for the East Marches. In 1535 a report commissioned by the Lord Warden tells us that 'Henry Collingwood is constable of Itall for term of his life, and dwelleth there four miles from Scotland, and may dispend 20 marks a year during his life in fee and annuity, and may serve the king of such lands as he has rule of with 30 horsemen. He is a true sharp borderer and keepeth a good house.' Above the arch of the gatehouse is a time-worn coat of the arms of the Manners family. Formerly a moat and drawbridge guarded the approach to the gatehouse; today we have two guns from the ill-fated *Royal George*; sunk near Spithead on 29 August 1782, with a loss of over 700 lives.

After Flodden the castle appears to have fallen into decline; today only the gatehouse, curtain wall, a tower and the keep remain. From the gatehouse a length of curtain wall some 3 feet thick, runs south-east to a tower, the basement of which is finely vaulted. The keep is now nothing more than a shell; but its main features are still traceable. It had a strongly groined basement supporting a room on the first floor, probably the kitchen, with a large fireplace. Above this were two additional floors, the hall, and reached by a newel-stair the bedrooms; a series of smaller rooms also had access from it. Some of the little traceried windows of two lights still remain. A portcullis may have defended the outer doorway; four holes in the north wall held the four wooden bars for when the gate was open. This was an unusual defence for so small a tower.

FORD CASTLE

Ford Castle is situated in one of the most romantic corners of the county – a corner that at one time was filled to the resounding beat of drums at Flodden Field; from the low ridge, it commands views over Flodden Field and the distant Cheviots. Although not actually on the border, like Wark and Norham, Ford played a major part in its defence of the Realm. In 1100 Ford was under Norman rule and part of the barony of Robert de Muschamp; Odinel de Ford was to build a manor house here when he married into the de Muschamps and granted the manor in the thirteenth century. Sir William Heron was to take possession of the castle when he married Mary, the daughter of Odinel de Ford. The mansion he was to build was licensed to crenellate in the reign of Edward III; this was a time when the Scots, inspired by their victory at Bannockburn, were becoming more and more daring in their incursions on English soil. Ten years earlier they had laid waste to Northumberland, coming to within 4 miles of Newcastle; later they were to treat Durham in a similar way. Encouraged by the king, barons all along the Border began to build their tower houses and curtain walls to defend their homes; as part of these defences the castle found itself in skirmishes on many occasions. One such dispute led to the imprisonment of William in 1387; and then later murdered in 1428 by John Manners of Etal. In the early sixteenth century John Heron, otherwise known as the 'Bastard', was to bring more trouble on to the family; feuds at this time were commonplace and settlements were often sought on truce days held by the Wardens of the Marches. It was on such a day that he and two associates murdered Sir Robert Ker, the Scottish Warden of the Middle March. The result of this was a feud that lasted until 1660. It was here at Ford that James IV, infatuated by the charms of the Lady Heron, spent some time before that fateful battle at Flodden, while Sir William Heron was at the time his prisoner in Fast Castle. James had become well known for his exploits with women, and Elizabeth Heron was known for her beauty. Lady Heron's reasons for taking part in this relationship were twofold: her wish for her husband's release and to protect her castle. After the battle Sir William was released in exchange for some of the Scottish prisoners that were taken at Flodden Field.

Originally the castle consisted of four towers joined by high curtain walls to form an inner court. The entrance was then on the west side. This pattern, first adopted in Northumberland is also to be seen at Chillingham, was to continue for 300 years. In 1761 Sir John Hussy Delaval made an attempt to rebuild the castle in the mock Gothic style that was stylish at the time; the result was the destruction of almost everything of interest except the two flanking towers. One hundred years later in 1861 Lady Waterford was to remove some of this work and a fountain designed by her stands in the grounds; but like her predecessor also destroyed she also some of the ancient stonework. The castle is now maintained by Northumberland County Council as a field study centre.

HARBOTTLE CASTLE

Harbottle Castle was built by the joint efforts of Henry II and the Bishop of Durham and at the time it was the most remote of all outposts. It stands on a natural ridge 9 miles west of Rothbury on the site of a Saxon stronghold. When viewed from Harbottle Crags or Clennell Street, it seems lost in the vastness of the area, yet from here it is clear why the site was chosen. The hill on which it stands has steep sides all round except to the east and overlooks the Coquet. In time it was to become one of the largest of the Northumbrian castles; it was also to be in control of the long line of Border defences. As part of his programme to replace all timber castles with stone, Henry II ordered Odinel de Umfraville to build his here in 1157. The motte was on the south side overlooking the village; on the west was the keep with a projecting entrance. The eastern half of the site was a barmkin under the observation and protection of the keep. A gate and gate tower control access to the bailey and another entrance on the west, within the walls, to the keep. In the inner bailey to the north-west of the keep are various foundations of some domestic buildings and a well. It was soon sacked by the Scots, and then rebuilt more strongly. A hundred years later they were to besiege it in vain. In 1319, following the Battle of Bannockburn, it was taken by Robert the Bruce and was supposed to have been dismantled, but this was not carried out. By 1515 it had been restored enough to receive Margaret Tudor, sister of Henry VIII for her confinement. It was here on 8 October, a few days after her arrival, that she gave birth to a daughter Margaret. Following the birth of her child Queen Margaret became very ill. She was moved by litter to Carrington Castle and then to Morpeth, the castle of Lord Dacre. By this time it was becoming more difficult to keep the castle in a good state of repair, and in 1543 a report stated 'it is in such decay that the garrison cannot now lodge in it without great peril'; the garrison at the time was eighty men. During the rein of Elizabeth I the castle was restored at a cost of 'two hundreth and fortye pound'; the garrison then being recorded as consisting of a hundred men and their officers, the latter receiving 4 shillings a day, while soldiers got 8d each. However, in 1558 thieves were to break into the castle and carry away goods that were stored inside. It was then that it became the residence for the Warden of the Middle Marches where they were to stay up until the late sixteenth century. In 1604 when King James ruled both kingdoms it was 'an old castle, much decayed', and he had no intention of restoring it. He granted all the Crown lands in Tynedale and Redesdale to a favourite called George Home; who went on to become the Earl of Dunbar. When the castle finally fell into ruin its stones were used to build a second castle; this was an impressive seventeenth-century house seen when approaching the village from the east. This dignified mansion was built by the Widderingtons.

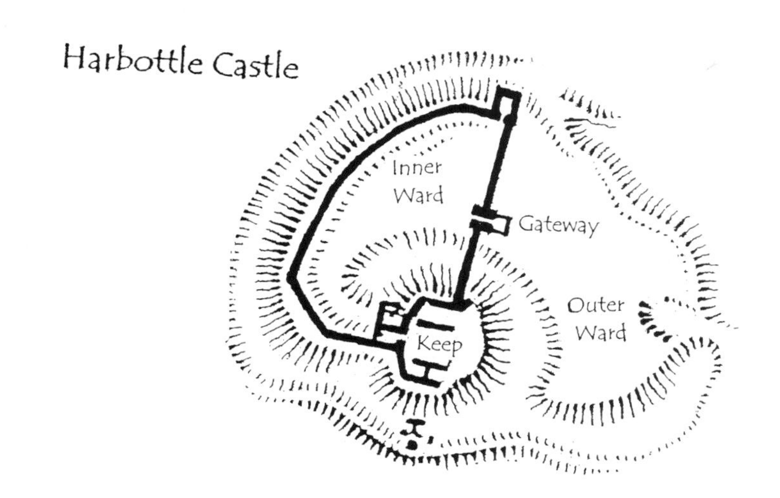

LINDISFARNE CASTLE

Crowning the cone-shaped volcanic mound known as Beblowe Crags, Lindisfarne Castle is one most distinct and picturesque features of the Island. The Earl of Hertford, brother of Jane Seymour, Henry VIII's third wife, built it as an artillery fort, using the stone from the then-dissolved Priory. The gun batteries were on two levels, approached from the south through a portcullis gate. In 1639 a visitor to the castle had this to say: 'There are twenty-four men and a captain kept in pay to man it, the common soldiers have 6d per day. The governor was Captain Rugg, famous for his generous and free entertainment; and for his great bottlenose.'

Although it saw little military action, its seizure in 1715 by two Jacobite Rebels was to bring some colour into its drab life; its capture came at a time when twelve of the fifteen men who garrisoned the castle were absent. On the evening of 10 October that year, Lancelot Errington, the master of a brigantine that was lying in the harbour, assisted by his nephew, seized the castle on behalf of James, exiled son of King James II. On the initial pretext of requiring a shave from the master gunner, he was to return to the castle with his nephew, gaining admission once more on the pretence of having lost the key of his watch. A struggle ensued that ended with the gunner and his sentries thrown out of the castle; they then hoisted the white flag of the 'Pretender' and signalled to the mainland for reinforcements but before they arrived a party of soldiers who had come to retake the fort made them their prisoners the next day. They were taken to Berwick gaol. With the help of outside friends Errington and his nephew burrowed themselves out, crossed the Tweed in a boat and fled to Bamburgh. They were hidden for nine days by a friend in the castle in a pea-stack and with a £500 reward on the older man's head, they made their way to Newcastle, from where they escaped to France.

By 1820 the castle's use as a fortification ceased with the removal of its garrison; it was then to serve as a coastguard station until the latter part of the century. In 1901 Edward Hudson, founder of *Country Life* magazine, negotiated its purchase; he then went on to commission Sir Edwin Lutyens to restore and convert it into a private house. Lying some 500 yards north of the castle are the castle gardens; the discovery in 1911 of the earlier Fort's garden planting plans were to make Gertrude Jekyll redesign them as part of its conversion. Both castle and garden are now in the hands of the National Trust.

NORHAM CASTLE

Standing on the English side of the River Tweed in an area known as Norhamshire in the palatine of Durham, Norham Castle was of major importance, for it guarded one of the primary fords over the Tweed. Bishop Flambard of Durham built it on the site of a motte-and-bailey castle in 1121. A constable appointed by the Bishop commanded it, and should the diocese become vacant this honour fell upon the King. In the early days Norham was as often in Scottish hands as much as the English and in the year 1200 William the Lion spent Lent in the castle and kept his fast by having fourteen kinds of fish. As may be expected of a Border fortress, its position ensured that it had its fair share of raids and in 1157 Henry II ordered the castles at Newcastle, Bamburgh and Wark-upon-Tweed to be rebuilt in stone. At the same time Hugh of Puiset, the Bishop of Durham, fortified the castle at Norham by building a stone keep. In 1215 Alexander, King of Scotland, was to besiege the castle for forty days without success. A century later in 1318 the Scots were to blockade Norham unsuccessful for a whole year; a second siege in the following year of seven months was equally in vain. It was during the second siege that the famous incident in Scott's 'Marmion' is supposed to have taken place. Sir Walter Marmion was a Lincolnshire knight, who, with a golden-crested helmet given to him by his lady, came to Norham to prove his love; she commanded of him that he was to seek 'the daungerest place in England'.

In 1513, while Henry VIII was invading France, Scotland crossed the Tweed and laid siege to Norham with some large Scottish cannon, including 'Mons Meg', which today stands in Edinburgh Castle. At the end of two days the barbican lay in ruins and the outer ward taken. The Scottish defeat at Flodden halted the invasion, and Norham was soon back in the hands of the English. It resisted repeated attacks during the thirteenth and fourteenth centuries, which made it seem to be impregnable; in the 1541 survey of Border strongholds Norham was reported as being 'in muche decay, the outer walls old, thynne and weak'. By the time the shires of Norham and Holy Island were taken from the See of Durham in 1559 the castle was no longer maintained. The Lord Warden reported to Lord Cecil in 1580 that

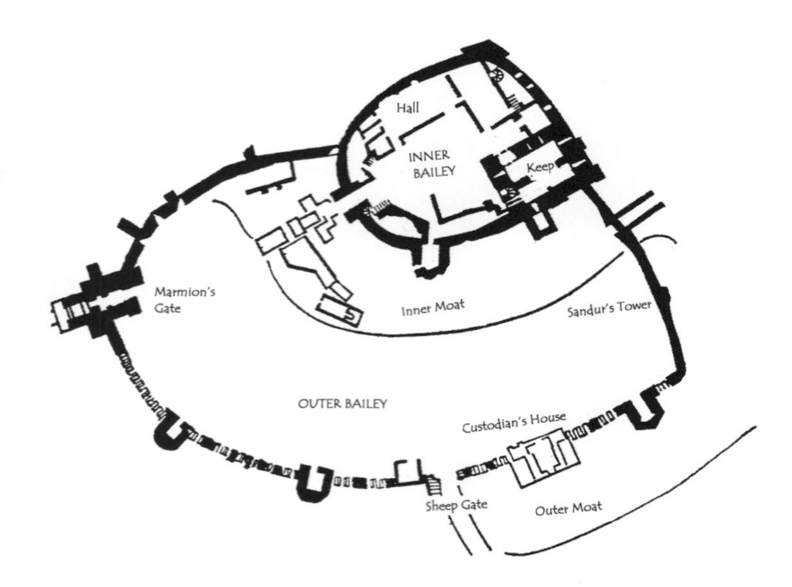

if 'speedy remedy be not had it will fall flat to the ground'. However, with no the need for a castle in the north, Queen Elizabeth I declared she would pay nothing for its restoration.

The west gate, or Marmion's Gate, is the main entrance and faces the road that runs down to the village. The outer ward is remarkably spacious in order to accommodate the large garrison stationed here. A wooden bridge on the site of its medieval predecessor is used to enter the inner bailey. Eastwards of Marmion's Gate we find that the curtain wall is pierced with portholes for small cannon – the latest form of defence. It was at the point where the curtain reaches the inner moat that a tunnel was made in 1495 for flooding the moat. The water was led in from a mill burn at the other end, and entered through the still visible channel called Bishop Fox's aqueduct. Dominating the north-east corner of the castle is the keep, protected by the steep banks of the River Tweed. Originally the keep was two storeys high with a barrel-vaulted basement, but this was raised in the fifteenth century by two further storeys, bringing the height to 90 feet. A cross wall was inserted in the basement to bear the increase in weight. An inner moat, crossed by a drawbridge, separates it from the outer ward, and yet another moat protects the outer bailey on its southern side. Along the southern curtain wall are the remains of the sheep gate, which cattle used to enter the castle. Norham, now in the care of English Heritage, ranks with Bamburgh and Dunstanburgh for being one of the great pictorial ruins in Northumberland.

PRESTON TOWER, CHATHILL

Preston Tower lies to the east of the Great North Road 8 miles north of Alnwick. Built by Sir Robert Harbottle, it is one of the few survivors of the seventy-eight pele towers listed in 1415. After fighting alongside Henry IV at the Battle of Otterburn, Harbottle became Sheriff of Northumberland and Constable of Dunstanburgh Castle. Pevsner tells us that it is a miniature edition of Langley Castle (see page 107), having a hall tower and four corner turrets. In 1603 two of its towers were demolished and the stone plundered to erect farm buildings and cottages. Not only is the basement in the south-west tower vaulted but also there are vaulted rooms in each of the three levels, which is unusual. And like most others in the tower, the door at the base is only 4 feet 9 inches high. For two and a half centuries the tower fell into decay; then, in 1864, Henry Baker Cresswell rescued it for the purpose of holding water tanks for his Georgian house next door.

The tower today, with its unaltered rooms, historical maps, diagrams, ballads and stories portrays a stark picture of the grim way of life under the constant threat of Border reivers.

PRIOR CASTELL'S TOWER, FARNE ISLANDS

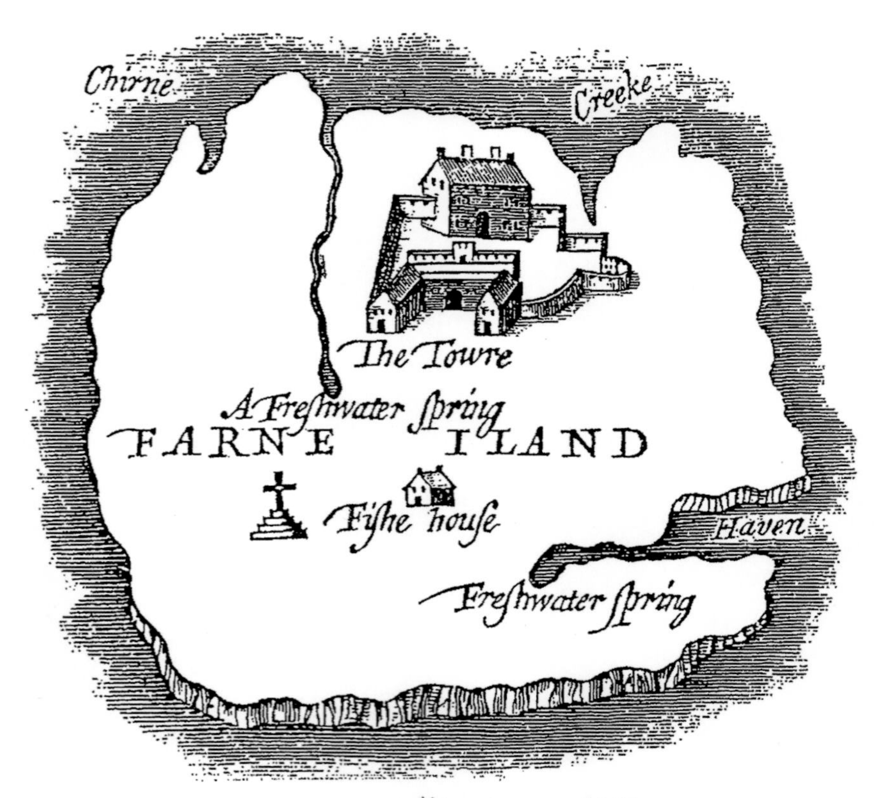

Prior Castell's Tower 1611

The Farne Islands are the most easterly of the great Whin Sill outcrop. Depending on the state of the tide there are between fifteen and twenty-eight islands; the largest is the Inner Farne. Thomas Castell, Prior of Durham, was to erect the tower on the island in the fifteenth century, possibly to replace an earlier building. Built as a Border pele, only three of the tower's four storeys now remain standing. In the tunnel-vaulted ground floor are the remains of the so-called Well of St Cuthbert. A steep mural stair serves both the first and second floors before it becomes a spiral to the roof in the south-east corner. On the first floor was the hall, with a fireplace and two garderobes and a trefoil-arched older feature. An eighteenth-century panelled wooden screen now divides up the room. In the mid-sixteenth century, after the Dissolution of the Monasteries, the tower was used as a fort, before it was converted to a lighthouse in the reign of Charles II. In 1848 the Venerable Charles Thorp, Archdeacon of Durham, was to restore the tower and gave the stair its splat balusters.

ROCK HALL, EMBLETON

Four miles to the north-east of Alnwick is the charming village of Rock. It was the de Rocks who held the manor here under the Barony of Alnwick. In time it was passed to the de Tughalls, the de Swinhoes, the Lawsons and the Salkelds; and their arms appear over a blocked doorway in front of the house together with three sundials and the date 1670. The most famous member of this family was Colonel John Salkeld, a loyal Royalist and committed to the Stuart cause. According to his epitaph in the nearby church, he served Charles I 'with a constant, dangerous and expensive loyalty as volunteer, captain and Colonel of horse'. In spite of his antics his career was never nearer to being cut short than when, at the age of twenty-seven, he murdered John Swinburne of Capheaton near the gates of Meldon, an incident in which he managed to escape punishment. A later owner of the hall, one John Fenwick, was involved in a similar affair when during a duel with Ferdinando Forster he treacherously stabbed his opponent as he lay on the ground. Not quite as fortunate as Salkeld, he was executed a month later. In 1549 the house was used as the headquarters for a band of Spanish mercenary troops under the command of Sir Julian Romero, who had been engaged to fight the Scots. The Scots at the time were being supported by French troops.

The central part of the building is a rectangular tower in shape and dates from the late thirteenth century. It is divided by an inner wall and had a smaller tower on the south side, with another tower about 20 feet square on the north side. The Salkelds added a manor house to the north side in the seventeenth century. The hall was gutted by fire in the eighteenth century and was to remain a ruin for over fifty years before being restored in 1809 by Charles Bosanquet; enlarged and restored, it was to retain the manor house and the pele tower from which it sprang.

WHITTINGHAM TOWER

Whittingham, sitting on the old coach road, is one of the most beautiful villages in the county; it takes on Blanchland for the title as being the perfect village. The main road from Morpeth to Wooler now runs 2 miles to the east. In the centre of the village, overlooking the wooded dene, rises the old pele tower; its rugged walls and casement windows paint a fine picture. Tomlinson tells us that the name is derived from 'the dwelling in the meadow' The tower, which originally belonged to the Heron family, passed to the Collingwoods and then the Ravensworths. It was Lady Ravensworth who restored this fortified house in the middle of the village and for more than 100 years the tower was an almshouse for the elderly. Surmounting the tower are corbelled battlements with an enlarged bartizan that at once carried a flagstaff. The original roof was quite different to that of today; it was double gabled and covered with red pantiles drained by projecting spouts and a defensive barmkin possibly shut in the few outbuildings round the base of the tower.

In days gone by Whittingham was famous for its fair. Today's the fair is far different, but for more than 100 years 'games' were held in a field by the pub on the Saturday nearest to St Bartholomew's Day.

Durham

AUCKLAND CASTLE

For 800 years the rich and powerful Prince Bishops of Durham had a residence here. The castle, lying on the outskirts of Bishop Auckland, was their favourite because of its nearness to their hunting grounds in Weardale. It began its life as a manor house in the days of Bishop Pudsey and was converted into a castle by Bishop Bek. The gatehouse in Castle Square, designed in 1760 by Sir Thomas Robinson for Bishop Trevor, is the main entrance to the park from the market place. The Lodge, with its battlemented front and big mullioned windows, was at one time a woollen factory. From the gateway runs a drive that separates the castle and its gardens from the park. A crenellated screen with open pointed arches, built in 1796 by James Wyatt for Bishop Barrington, hides the garden, beyond which stands the bold and rugged pile of the castle. Every 200 years the castle has been altered in some way and each change was to emphasise the Bishop's role. The Prince Bishop was more than just head of the diocese; he was part-churchman, part-soldier and part-politician, reigning over the northern province on behalf of the king. It was to remain as an episcopal residence

up until the reign of Charles I. Following the Civil War it was confiscated and sold to Sir Arthur Hazelrigg, who immediately pulled down its two chapels and other parts of the castle to build a new mansion in the courtyard. With the return to the old order after the Restoration, John Cosin was appointed to the See of Durham. He demolished what Hazelrigg had constructed and spent an enormous sum restoring the castle to its former glory; it was to commence with the building of a great new chapel out of the aisled hall, and later bishops, each in their turn, carried out further improvements. The glorious Chapel of St Peter is reputed to be the largest private chapel in Europe; it is one of the finest examples of its kind. John Langstaffe, a local mason, was to do the exterior work. Wyatt's porch forms the entrance to the house and stairs lead to the staterooms on the first floor. At the top of the staircase we pass through the octagonal ante-room with its gothic niches and plaster vault into the Throne Room. This contains the Great Throne, with its ogee-topped niche designed by Wyatt. Lawrence portraits of Shute Barrington and William Van de Mildert, the last two Prince Bishops, have their place of honour on either side of the wide fireplace, and around the walls are the many faces of other past prelates. A door in the south wall leads to an adjoining room known as the Long Dining Room; Bishops Ruthall and Tunstall built it in the sixteenth century. This room owes its decoration to Bishop Trevor. On its walls are a series of canvases that depict Jacob and his sons; these were painted by Zurbaran in 1640.

One of the works by Benjamin, and commissioned by Bishop Trevor, is an eighteenth-century copy by Arthur Pond. The King Charles Room, with Bishop Trevor's crest at each corner, is a reminder of that unhappy king. He came here on three occasions. The first was when he was Prince of Wales; the second as a guest of Bishop Morton while on his way to Scotland; the third was as a prisoner on 4 February 1647.

The magnificent chapel, which was transformed by Cosin's from the Great Hall into a place of worship, is attached to the main block at its extreme north-east angle. One of the greatest changes he made was to raise its central roof; this was to provide a clerestorey. The ceiling is as he left it, with his coat of arms and those of the diocese on many of the panels. At the west end of the building is the beautiful open screen, made and erected in March 1664. The two carpenters who were appointed to carry out the work were to be paid 40 shillings per yard, a yard being confirmed as 3 feet wide by 11 high. He died in 1672 and was buried on 29 April in the chapel that he loved and had so richly decorated. A huge inscribed slab covers his grave in the centre of the nave. The organ and loft were set up by his successor, Bishop Crewe. He was to appoint the King's organ maker, Bernard 'Father' Smith to carry out the work in 1688. The organ, built with a single keyboard, contained six complete stops and was all within a finely carved case of oak. But by the end of the nineteenth century it was in a state of collapse and Arthur Harrison of Harrison & Harrison of Durham was called in to advise; they were then contracted to rebuild it in 1903. The work cost £300.

In 1767 Bishop Trevor, as part of his alterations to the house and grounds, built a castellated deer enclosure. Gothic in style, it can be found a short distance from the castle. It has a grassed quadrangle with shelter in the arcades for the deer, which used to roam the park. A tall tower on the west side had an upper room in which the bishop and his guests could rest from hunting and allowed viewing the animals. It was here, in this park, that the English army gathered prior to the Battle of Neville's Cross in 1346.

Although it is now accepted as a castle, in the true sense of the word this was not always the case; and today's impression is of an episcopalian palace, which it has always been.

BARNARD CASTLE

This ancient fortress, whose imposing ruins are perched on a rock outcrop on the north bank of the Tees, appears to rise almost vertically from the river edge; it was here in the early part of the twelfth century that Bernard de Baliol first fortified this site after William II had granted it to him. Beneath its towers the town of Barnard Castle sprang into being. It has been a rendezvous point for both the famous and infamous though all the pages of its history; people such as Guy de Baliol, Guy Beauchamp, Richard Nevill and Richard III have all inhabited it at one time or another. The Baliols were to make their mark on British history. Guy de Baliol's great grandson was to found Balliol College, Oxford, and his son John was to become King of Scotland for a few years. The relationship between John de Baliol and his wife provides us with one of the most touching love stories recorded. On his death she had his heart embalmed and placed in a casket to carry with her at all times; she then built Sweetheart Abbey near Dumfries as his memorial. At her death in 1290 the casket was buried with her in the abbey. Following John de Baliol's death the estates passed in turn to three of his sons; the last, who was also named John, succeeded in 1278. With his death the era of the Baliols of Barnard Castle came to an end. All through the Middle Ages the castle's ownership had been the subject of a long-standing feud with the Bishops of Durham. In 1296 Antony Bek, Bishop of Durham, seized the castle and its lands to claim back the feudal rights for the bishopric. However, in the course of time he was to fall foul of Edward I, who seized the revenues of the bishopric and also that of the lordship of Barnard Castle in 1306. In 1307 Edward was to grant the lordship of Barnard Castle to Guy de Beauchamp, who was the Earl of Warwick. Save for a slight break it was in the possession of the Beauchamps for five generations though it is doubtful if the family ever used the castle as a residence; for the Balliols, it had been their principal residence, but to the Beauchamps it was of no consequence. In 1449 the Earldom of Warwick and the lordship of Barnard Castle then passed to Richard Nevill through his marriage to Anne, the sister of the last of the Beauchamp line. He became known in history as 'Warwick the Kingmaker', and was to play a key role in the Wars of the Roses. Their daughter Anne married Edward, Prince of Wales, who died at Tewksbury in 1471. She then went on to marry Richard III, with whom she had been educated at Middleham Castle. Marrying Anne was to give Richard the rights to the Earl of Warwick's northern estates. In 1477 he obtained a licence to found an ecclesiastical college in the castle for a dean and twelve secular priests, ten clerks and six choristers, but this does not appear to have been carried out.

One of most dramatic moments in the castle's history occurred in 1569, during the reign of Elizabeth I. The castle was to remain important until the 'Rising in the North', which was plotted at the nearby Raby Castle. In November 1569 supporters of Mary Queen of Scots were to lay siege to it. Garrisoned by Sir George Bowes of Streatlam, it was, at the time, Crown property. He was to resist all attacks until treachery and desertion forced him to surrender after eleven days, 'for want of provisions, upon honourable terms being allowed to depart with arms, ammunition and baggage'. Later he was to describe conditions during the siege.

> There had been a greatt want of bread, drynck, and water: which was our only drynk, save I mixed yt with some wyne. I fownde the people in the castle in continuall mutenyes, seeking not only, by greatt numbers, to leap the walls and run to the rebells, but also by all menes to betraye the castle to the rebells. So far, as in one daye and nyght, two hundred and twenty six men leapyd over the walls and opened the gaytes, and went to the enemy; off which number, thirty five broke their necks, legges or armes in leaping.

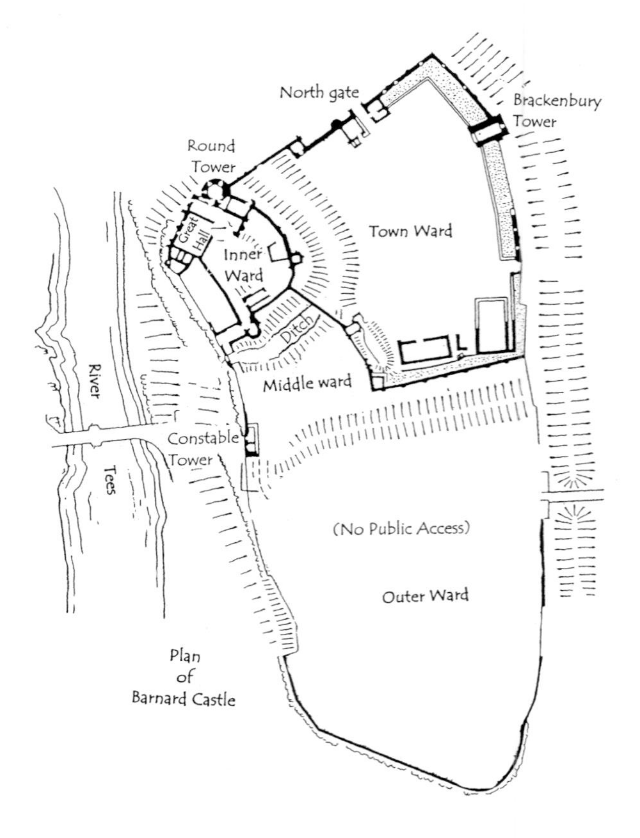

On his death some years later, and in recognition of his loyalty, Queen Elizabeth granted a lease of the castle to his family. In the Civil War it was again held by the Crown and came under siege from Cromwell; after a severe cannonade it was forced to surrender.

Robert Carr, a favourite to James I, was then awarded the castle, but it was returned to the Crown after his imprisonment for his complicity in the poisoning of Sir Thomas Overbury. Eventually it was sold to Sir Henry Vane, who was Secretary of State to Charles I. Sir Henry Vane was to dismantle the castle to provide material for the rebuilding of Raby this and the gradual and progressive decay has affected all but the outer shell. An unusual feature of the castle is that it had four wards, or baileys, although only the town ward and inner ward have much to show. Entrance to the castle is via the North Gate. This leads into the Town Ward, which served as a place of refuge when marauders were about. On the curtain wall to the east is the Brackenbury Tower. This was named after Sir Richard Brackenbury, one time constable of the Tower of London. Its barrel-vaulted undercroft served as both storage and

living quarters. A wooden bridge, to the south-west of the Town Ward, gives access across what was the moat to the smallest of the castles wards, the Middle Ward. The Constable Tower standing in the south-west corner of the Middle Ward housed the gate that linked it with the Outer Ward. The castle's Inner Ward was its heart, and the Great Hall and other buildings were arranged round its west curtain wall above the cliffs. Their windows are still to be seen in the wall. Straddling the curtain wall of the inner ward is the balliol, or round tower, which is the best-preserved part of the castle. One of the unusual features of the tower is the triangular spur at its base that continues upward until it blends with the rounded surface. This is from an earlier keep that was incorporated into the present one. Its condition, as with other buildings in the ward, is due to the vandalism of Sir Henry Vane in Cromwell's day. Within its 10-foot-thick walls are mural stairs, passages and garderobes. The basement is notable for its circular ceiling; it is formed of undressed stones laid in a rising spiral that results in a shallow dome, with its middle only 18 inches higher than the outer edge. Also to be found here is the indispensable castle well. The principal entrance to the tower is on the first floor and the apartment there with a fine two-lighted window and a fireplace was the State Room. From one of the window recesses a mural stair within the outer wall climbs to the ramparts giving access on the way to the upper floors. Though the Great Chamber next to the keep has disappeared, its remaining west wall retains one of the castle's most striking features: the big oriel window that used to form part of the upper floor. Supported by rows of corbels, it has five lights separated by mullions and was constructed while Richard, Duke of Gloucester, owned the castle. We have a keen reminder of him here on one of the large stones in the roof of the window; his device of a 'bristly boar' is carved within an interlacing border.

It is unfortunate that so much of this historic castle should have been deliberately, vandalised. What is fortunate is that what remains is now being preserved by English Heritage.

BELLISTER CASTLE

One mile south-west from the Haltwhistle to Featherstone road one comes close to Bellister Castle, on the summit of a low motte. The moat that once surrounded it dried up long ago and its contours now lost in the passage of time; the mound on which the ruin now stands may have been the remains of a motte-and-bailey castle from the eleventh century. In the Border survey of 1415 and 1541 it is described as a bastle house, a term that indicates that it was more than likely to have been a pele, and the name castle seems hardly warranted. When, in the sixteenth century, the Blenkinsopps came here, the tower had already been in existence for some time.

The legend of Bellister Castle concerns the haunting by the spirit of the 'Grey Man', whose life was hurried from this world in the following gruesome manner. In the days of the Border reivers Lord Blenkinsopp was very wary of strangers, but one evening in exchange for some tales and songs he allowed a travelling minstrel to shelter. As the evening wore on, the Lord grew increasingly suspicious of the minstrel and in the middle of the night he called his steward to check. Finding his bed was empty the Lord immediately ordered a search party with hunting dogs. It was not long until the dogs uncovered the minstrel on the banks of the Tyne and tore him to pieces. To this day Bellister has been haunted by the ghost of a man in grey with a pallid face, cut across by a bloody gash.

In the nineteenth century John Dobson rebuilt part of the castle, and following a fire in 1901 made more changes. This is a Scheduled Monument and Grade I listed building protected by law.

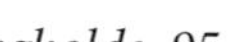

BLANCHLAND GATEHOUSE

Little more than a handful of cottages huddle round the square of this ancient hamlet, which was once the site of a Premonstratensian Abbey. It was in 1165, that Walter de Bolbec invited twelve White Canons of an order known for its strictness and self-denial, to settle on the banks of the River Derwent. They built an abbey and named it after the order's birthplace, Blanche Land in Normandy. In the nineteenth century, when a bridge was built over the river, a new road was made that passed through the archway of the abbey's gatehouse; the abbey precincts were entered through this gatehouse. As was the custom, visitors to the abbey would probably use the large room on the first floor. All the windows have hood moulds and are on the southern side for protection. Today, the small village post office is part of the old monastic gateway. Across the road from the gatehouse is the Lord Crewe Arms. Although now a pub, the Lord Crewe Arms was once the residence of the Abbot of Blanchland Abbey. With its dark vaulted basement it is thought to have been built in the thirteenth century. It also boasts two big fireplaces from the canons' kitchen and a priest hole in the chimney.

By 1623 the estates were falling into decline and the Forsters of Bamburgh purchased these from the Radcliffes. Lord Crewe, Bishop of Durham, then married Dorothy, the heiress to the estates of Bamburgh and Blanchland, and after paying off the mortgages of the debt-ridden estates he set up a charitable trust to administer them. In the mid-eighteenth century the trustees used stones from the abbey ruins to rebuild the village we see today.

BOWES CASTLE

Bowes is a bleak place; it stands on high ground and commands a good view of the land all around, much as the Roman fort of Lavatrae would have done some two thousand years ago. It is the site of a fort going back to the early part of the third century; Bowes, or Lavatrae as it was then known, guarded a fork in the east–west road across the northern wilderness. It was built in the latter part of the twelfth century by a loyal servant of Henry II named Richard the Engineer. Standing within the protection of the curtain walls the keep was more of a garrison post than that of a residential castle. A forebuilding protected the east side entrance, which was as the custom, on the first floor of the building. This was where the Great Hall stood with its conveniently adjoining kitchen. Large round-headed windows with set back jambs lighted the hall. On the first floor, a round-arched north doorway has set-back voussoirs flanked by small round-arch openings, while in the south-east corner are the remains of what was once a mural stair.

Although the keep is ruinous it is still impressive. It stands like a solitary sentinel to guard the northern outposts. There are traces of both inner and outer baileys to the south.

BRANCEPETH CASTLE

The pastoral village of Brancepeth lies about 5 miles south-west of the City of Durham. So secret is this place that to this day the castle remains hidden among its woods. It stands in a beautiful park with a fourteenth-century church for company, above the steeply wooded banks of Stockley Beck. The trees here are all that remains of the once great West Wood that supplied the timber for the Navy's first three-decker ship, the *Sovereign of the Seas*. Some 1,400 trees were felled and sent to Woolwich for its making. A broad drive leads to the gateway, flanked by two round towers that look like giant chess pieces, and enters into the spacious courtyard enclosed by lofty walls. The original building is supposed to have been pre-Conquest, and may have been the first castle in the county of Durham to have been embattled. Its foundations have been ascribed to the Bulmers, who owned the estate prior to the Norman invasion. Soon after it passed by the marriage of a Bulmer heiress to the Nevills, and Ralph Nevill, 1st Earl of Westmorland, is credited with its building. In 1537, for his taking part in the 'Pilgrimage of Grace', Sir John Bulmer was committed to the Tower; he was hanged and beheaded at Tyburn on 25 May. It was to remain with the Nevills until one fateful day in 1569. On the evening of 14 November the Earl assembled all the men at arms he could muster and made his way to his stronghold at Brancepeth. With a force that numbered only 1,500 men-at-arms, Charles Nevill, 6th Earl of Westmorland, was to set out from Brancepeth Castle on the ill-fated 'Rising of the North'. When news of this revolt reached the ears of Queen Elizabeth, she was incensed:

> The newes unto London came in all the speede that ever might be, and word is brought to our Royale Queene of the rising in the north countrie. Her grace she turned round about, and like a Royall Queen swore, 'I will ordayne them such a breakfast as never was seen in the north before'.

Such were the events of the day that many of the great houses were swept away and their various estates dispersed. After the northern rising the Crown was to hold the castle at Brancepeth until 1613, when James I granted it to Robert Carr, whom he had created Baron of Brancepeth and Earl of Somerset. When Carr was accused of poisoning Sir Thomas Overbury in 1615 the castle was again forfeit to the Crown when he was sent to prison. It was then to go through several hands before it was passed in trust into the hands of Ralph Cole, the wealthy Gateshead blacksmith. It was his grandson Ralph, who, because of his interest in the fine arts, so impoverished himself that he sold the castle in exchange for £16,000, and annuities for life for both he and his wife. The new owner was Sir Henry Bellasyse, whose daughter is forever remembered in North Country folklore as being the sweetheart of 'Bonnie' Bobbie Shafto, who lived at nearby Whitworth Hall. After three generations of occupation the estates passed into the hands of an heiress of the family; she was to bequeath the estate to the Earl of Fauconberg, a relative who promptly sold it on to John Tempest of Wynyard. At the time the estate was 4,000 acres of freehold tenure and the yearly rental was £2,134-8s-4d. It was then purchased by William Russell, who at once set about its rebuilding. The decision was regrettable. But even more regrettable was the choice of John Patterson of Edinburgh as architect; though he had a weakness for the Gothic style he knew little of antiquity. He died in the January of 1850; and without a male heir, his estate passed to his sister Emma, who in 1828 had married the eldest son of the Viscount Boyne. Almost a hundred years later it was to become the headquarters of the Durham Light Infantry, who remained there until its closure.

DILSTON CASTLE

The most wretched figure in all of Northumberland's past is James Radcliffe, the 3rd Earl of Derwentwater. He was born, the grandson of Charles II, in 1689, and sent with his cousin James III to be educated at St Germain's. It was because of James that the young Earl was to lose his life and lands. In the fateful year of 1715 the Earl's wife was to persuade him, against his better judgement, to ride with the supporters of James Stuart. A Stuart himself, and brought up at the court of the exiled James II, he would need little persuasion. Both he and his brother Charles joined the Jacobite rising against King George I; both were captured. It was in consequence to his Stuart blood and the fact that he was a Roman Catholic that predestined his harsh end. In 1716 James Radcliffe was to give up his life to the headsman on Tower Hill; it was on a cold morning in February. Now only the ruined tower remains of the glories that were once Dilston.

> And when the head that wears the crown,
> Shall be laid low like mine,
> Some honest hearts may then lament
> For Radcliffe's fallen line.
> Farewell to pleasant Dilston Hall,
> My father's ancient seat;
> A stranger now must call thee his,
> Which gars my heart to greet.

In 1868, a woman named Amelia was to camp in the ruins and claim she was the great granddaughter of John Radcliffe. When challenged she replied that she was the Countess of Derwentwater, the real owner and possessor. There she was to take some furniture into the only room with four walls and covered a corner of it with a tarpaulin. Beneath this canopy she was to compose the most eloquent of letters. 'I found not a voice to cheer me; nothing but naked, plasterless walls; a hearth with no frame of iron; the little chapel, which contains the sacred tombs of the silent dead, and the dishonoured ashes of my Grand-sires.' In 1805, this 'little chapel' held the tombs of the Radcliffes and the coffin of the 3rd Earl had been opened for the purpose of identification; but by some thoughtlessness the vault was not resealed. The body was put on display for some days and the teeth were in fact drawn and sold as mementos by the village blacksmith.

The tranquil beauty of this site, combined with the story of the ill-fated Earl, has led over the years to a string of poems and novels.

DURHAM CASTLE

There are two kings in England, namely the Lord King of England wearing a crown in sign of his regality, and the Lord Bishop of Durham wearing a mitre in place of a crown as a symbol of his regality in the Bishopric of Durham.
Steward of the Bishopric, 1302

There are not many English castles that are so superbly placed as that at Durham; with the magnificent Norman cathedral, it forms the centrepiece on an oval plateau that is almost enclosed, as if by a moat, in a bend of the river. Set high above, impregnably remote, almost 1,000 old, despotic in its ecclesiastical history, it remains a symbol of what England was, what it used to do, and how it used to suffer, as well as survive. It is a scene worth gazing upon from every vantage point.

It was in 1069 that William the Conqueror came to inspect this rocky site high above the river and determined to make it the centre of the palatine. Built in 1072 to protect the governor, the bishop and the church, it was, until the mid-nineteenth century, the main seat of the Bishops of Durham. Unique in English history, the Prince Bishops ruled the county palatine; they held full royal rights within the bishopric; they levied taxes, had their own exchequer, struck their own coins, appointed their own judges, gave charters to towns, licensed fairs, had their own assembly of parliament and could mete out the death penalty or in the case of treason or felonies give pardons. They had admiralty rights all along the coast of the bishopric, and had the royal privilege of claiming wrecked ships, sturgeons and whales that washed up. In exchange for these privileges the bishop had to maintain an army to keep the Scots out. For more than four centuries the castle was to prove time and again how impregnable it was. Bishops such as Hugh Pudsey, Ranulf Flambard and Antony Bek controlled both the affairs of the bishopric and those of the nation. The men they employed were known as the Haliwerfolf or the 'people of the saint', and not liable for service outside the boundaries of the bishopric. The early city occupied the ground, now known as the Palace Green, that lay between the castle and the cathedral, but in the ensuing years it was cleared of its dwellings and the castle became the separate entity it is today. It was

here where women scolds were to suffer for the glibness of their tongues, feuds were to be settled by armed combat, public hangings took place, and where the great Corpus Christi procession assembled.

Durham is the shape of a typical motte-and-bailey castle: that is, it has its keep on the mound at one side of the bailey and the inner buildings enclosed by walls. East of the castle lies a narrow street of houses called The Bailey, a name that implies a defensive role. Along its length are the churches of St Mary le Bow and St Mary the Less. The approach to the castle entrance is by way of the Palace Green. At one time this was guarded by a barbican and drawbridge. Its features are Norman; heavy oak doors, studded ironwork and massive bolts are all more than 500 years old. In 1800 James Wyatt was to add the Gothic look to it for Bishop Barrington. The changes that Wyatt was to make have been variously described as 'in the worst possible taste', 'barbarous' and 'romantic', leaving it to the layman to make his own appraisal. On the right from within the courtyard is the terraced motte of the octagonal keep. Said to have been built by

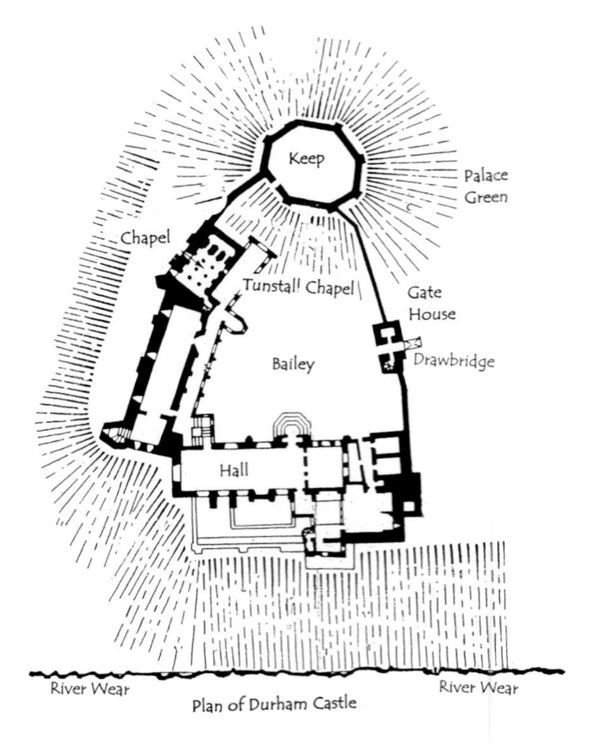

Plan of Durham Castle

William the Conqueror, it occupies the summit on the north side of Palace Green. On the west of the courtyard is the Great Hall, built about 1300 by Bishop Bek. The original pointed doorway built by Bek leads into one of the most splendid dinning halls in England. Pevsner tells us 'it need not fear comparison with the grandest halls of Oxford and Cambridge'. And it was here that Sir Walter Scott and the Duke of Wellington sat down to dinner on 3 October 1827 with the last of the Prince Bishops, William Van Mildert. Scott was to record the event and tells us:

> We dined in the old baronial hall, impressive from its rude antiquity, and fortunately free from the plaster of former improvement, as I trust it will long be from the gingerbread taste of modern Gothicizers. The bright moon streaming in through the old Gothic windows contrasted strangely with the artificial lights within; spears, banners and armour were intermixed with the pictures of old bishops, and the whole had a singular mixture of baronial pomp with the grave and more chastened dignity of prelacy.

Armour and flags adorn the walls together with rows of portraits of bishops and other benefactors. The kitchen, next to the Hall, was where huge feasts were prepared. Still in use today, it is a big room with a high louvered roof and huge fireplaces. Bishop Fox had it converted from a Norman guardroom. Beyond the Great Hall a room leads to one of the castles most striking features: the Black Staircase. This is among the finest of its kind in the country. The work of Bishop Cosin, it rises through four storeys round a square open well and is of black oak with pierced panels of willow carved with foliage. It connects Bishop Tunstall's Gallery to the Pudsey Gallery above. Originally only the outer walls supported the staircase, but this proved to be inadequate and the Tuscan columns were added to correct the outward slope of the tread. The Tunstall Gallery, with its mullioned windows, was built to provide access to the new chapel. The oldest part of the castle is the Norman crypt, where, in spite of the poor light, you may distinguish odd carvings; it reminds one of the churches in France, where such designs are common. Here in Durham the craftsmen were superior, but the inspirations seemed to have been the same: a humorous twist in the mind of the artist, a desire to illustrate the conventional with some jokes of his own. A seventeenth-century maintenance account tells us: 'To the plumber for soldering in the great chapel, the little chapel, and in other chambers, for ten days, at 5d per day, total cost 4s-2d.' One of the grandest

apartments is the Senate Room which was formerly the Bishop's drawing room. It is hung with sixteenth-century Flemish tapestry that shows the life of Moses; the Elizabethan style fireplace here dates from 1603 when James I stayed here on his way to London to be crowned.

As seen today the castle integrates different dates; and each of the bishops has left his mark on the surrounding buildings by carving his personal coat-of-arms into the stonework. In the early nineteenth century, Bishop Van Mildert gave up the castle; retaining only a couple of rooms for himself, he endowed part of his revenue of £40,000 a year to found the University.

'This city is celebrated in the whole Empire of the Britons.' So begins an Anglo-Saxon poem of Durham; today it is no less celebrated.

FEATHERSTONE CASTLE

Featherstone is one of the most striking castles in Northumberland; Bates was to describe it as being 'perhaps the loveliest tower in the county with its corner bartizans and carved corbels'. It sits in seclusion, close to the ford, on the south bank of the south Tyne about 3 miles south-west of Haltwhistle. It is said that the name comes from the Fueder Stones, an ancient megalith that was built by placing a fourth stone across three uprights. The first recorded owner for the manor at Fetherstanhishaln was one Helias de Featherstonehaugh; he was resident here in the eleventh century. Oddly enough it does not appear on the 1415 list of strongholds; in 1541 the survey tells us that 'At Feeatherstonhaughe ys a toure of thinherytaunce of Alexander Featherstonhaughe of the same in good rep'ac'ons'.

It was in the fourteenth century that Thomas de Featherstonehaugh built a tower here; with its vaulted basement and decorated doorway it is typical of its time. Keeping to its castellated style a further three towers were added to it at a later date. A castellated wall surrounds the lawns and gardens. In the sixteen century, Richard Featherstonehaugh was to become chaplain to Catherine of Aragon, but because of his loyalty to the Pope and Henry VIII's first wife he was executed.

The family were often involved in Border raids and local feuds, including an affray with the Ridleys, and the death of Sir Albany Featherstonehaugh in 1530 was the result of these feuds. To this day the site of this murder is still known as Deadman's Haugh, which lies about a mile from the castle across the river. Surtees was to write a ballad about the event.

Hoot awa' lads, hoot awa'.
Hae ye heard how the Ridleys and Thirwalls and a',
Ha' set upon Albany Feathersonehaugh,
And taken his life at the Deadmanshaugh?
There was Willemotewick,
And Hardriding Dick'
And Hughie of Harden, and Will of the Wa',
I cannot tell a', I cannot tell a',
And money a mair that the de'il may knaw.

The auld man went down, but Nicol his son
Ran away afore the fight was begun;
And he run, and he run,
And afore they were done,
There was many a Featherston gat sic a stun,
As never was seen since the world begun.

Hoot, hoot, the auld man's slain outright!
Lay him out now wi' his face down: he's a sorrowful sight.
Janet thou donot,
I'll lay my best bonnet,
Thou get's a new gude-man afore it be night.

As for so many families, the Civil War was to prove the undoing of the Featherstonehaughs. Like many Northumbrians they were to lose their estates when they supported Charles I; but a Featherstonehaugh who was mayor of Newcastle bought these back in 1711. His son, however, once he had inherited an estate in Sussex, sold it on to James Wallace. It was to remain with his family until it became a school during the Second World War. The present owner is Colonel John Clark, who purchased the castle in 1961.

Like many other castles in Northumberland, it has a ghost or ghosts. The story is that in an old house at Hardriding lived a certain Hugh Ridley, who was in love with the heiress of Featherstone. The heiress's father however had other ideas about a bridegroom for his daughter, and the girl was married to her horror to a far off cousin.

Following the ceremony, the guests and bride set out on a hunt in the nearby woods. However, they were ambushed by the heiress's lover and his friends, and the whole party was killed. In the confusion of the *mêlée* the bride too was slain, and overcome with grief the lover killed himself. In the meantime, the bridal breakfast had been prepared as the Baron awaited the return of his guests. It was not until midnight that the door opened and in staggered a bloodstained bridegroom and guests, taking their seats in silence. To his horror the Baron realised that these were ghosts, and as he felt a cold blast sweep across the hall, the bridal party faded away. It is said that every year at the same time of day the ghostly bridal party may be seen riding in the castle woods.

HEXHAM OLD GAOL

The ancient market town of Hexham in the fertile Tynedale valley was once a constant target for the Scots, for, like many of England's Border towns, it was not walled. It was in 1330 that William Melton, Archbishop of York, ordered his receiver at Hexham, Thomas Fox, to construct a gaol. He wrote to him saying 'We wish and order you to have made a good and strong gaol, in which our prisoners can be securely held and guarded and the expenses incurred in the building of this we will allow out of your account.' This was the first building in England to be specially built for this purpose and was used as such up to the early nineteenth century. In 1332 he wrote again informing him:

> We wish and order you to repair our gaol at Hexham and to provide shackles, manacles, fetters and other items necessary to the repair of the goal and the guarding of the prisoners. Wherefore we appoint John de Cawood, barber, bearer of these letters, sergeant of our manor and town of Hexham and keeper of the gaol. And we wish that you will allow the said John for his salary and expenses as was automany the sum of two pence a day.

It was used to house reivers accused of committing crimes within the Border Marches. Trials would be held here every three months. However, punishments were so severe that prisoners were often found not guilty to save them from the death penalty. Despite this, many a bold Northerner twiddled his thumbs here while awaiting execution.

The building itself is oblong in shape with triple corbels that in the past would have carried a parapet and machicolations. It has two vaulted chambers on the ground floor and one room on each of the two upper storeys. A trapdoor was the only way to reach the vaulted dungeons in the basement. The gaol was in use until 1828, when a new county jail was built at Morpeth, and the Hexham House of Correction was used for petty thieves. It was then used as a bank, a solicitor's office, a rifle club, a billiards hall and finally a place to fire watch during the Second World War. By the mid-1970s the building was in a bad state, and the Historic Hexham Trust proposed a scheme for its repair; major restoration would have to be done if the building were to be reopened. It was not until 1980 that it opened its doors as a Tourist Information Centre and Museum. The installation of a glass lift gave access to all floors, as well as a view of the dungeon with its 20-foot drop; also to be reinstated was the gaol's spiral staircase after it had been partially removed in the Victorian era. In the museum the displays gives the visitor an insight into the days of the Border reiver and the life that they led.

HYLTON CASTLE

Hylton Castle stands, with its turreted shield-hung front, about 3 miles west of Sunderland. Its battlemented figures and triple rows of old-style windows give it an imposing façade. For more than six centuries Hylton Castle was the home of the Hylton family, one of the oldest and most powerful families in the county of Durham. At one time this great and ancient family held manors in Hylton, Durham, York and Northumberland. The original castle was rectangular in shape and measured some 75 × 45 feet and four storeys in height. Its west front is a mirror image of the east front of Lumley Castle (see page 110) in the arrangement of its turrets. In addition to the two that flank the entrance there is one at each of the corners. The turrets are crowned with octagonal battlemented and machicolated parapets that were at one time adorned by stone warriors. Above the main entrance a wealth of medieval heraldry is to be seen. The bulk of them are in the central bay. Here we can see the devices of Nevill, Percy, Hylton, Lumley, Greystoke, Eure, Washington, Ogle, Conyers and many others. A turret projecting from the east face bears the arms of Richard II. The coat of arms for the Washingtons carries three stars and two bars and it is believed that George Washington adapted the coat of arms to design the Stars and Stripes; the shield earned its place here because a Baron of Hylton was to marry into that family. At the top of one of the turrets is a banner that bears the Royal Arms; it also bears the arms of France, as it first appeared on the Great Seal of Henry V, who was to lay claim to the French throne after the battle of Agincourt. A central passage flanked by vaulted chambers on either side ran through to a rear courtyard. At the rear end of the passage a doorway led to the foot of the main newel stair. Still intact, it spirals up to the battements and gives access to all the floors. An usual feature of the battlements was the provision

of shallow stone troughs; these could carry boiling liquids to the machicolations without exposing the defenders into the view of the enemy below. The first floor was occupied by the Great Hall and solar, with kitchen, buttery and pantry attached. Opening from the hall was the room known as the solar, or private apartment, to which the lord and his family could readily withdraw. The chamber at roof level had a loophole through which the battlements were viewed. War seems to have been the pleasure of the Hyltons: one was killed in Kent, one in Normandy, one in France, three in the Holy Wars, one at Agincourt, three at the Battle of Bordeaux, five at Market Bosworth and four at Flodden Field. Over the years a total of twenty-one are recorded.

In the sixteenth century descendants were to be found in the employment of the monarchy; one William Hylton is recorded as body tailor to Henry VIII and one of his daughters as seamstress in the court of Elizabeth I. Praiseworthy though it was as a stronghold, it slowly fell into disuse and towards the end of Elizabeth's reign was reported to in a state of neglect. In 1700 the gatehouse was to become the basis for a large house that was to be built in two phases: John Hylton added a north wing in the early eighteenth century, and this was followed by a matching south wing shortly after. Hylton Castle has long been the haunt of an unfortunate servant killed by one of the Barons of Hylton. The Baron had ordered his horse, and being impatient went to the stable and found the young boy asleep. In his rage he struck the young boy with what was to prove to be a deadly blow with a scythe. After covering the body of his victim with straw he threw it into the pond that was near by, where, some months later, the young boy's skeleton of was found.

The ballad of 'The Cau'd Lad of Hylton' tells how the murdered youth, Roger Skelton, used to pace round the castle hall, with his head literally in his hand, singing, 'soft and low':

> Hylton's line dishonoured fall;
> Lay with the dust proud Hylton's walls,
> Murder blots the household sword;
> Strip the lands from Hylton's lord.

This story is said to have its origins in the coroner's inquest on the body of Roger Skelton held on 3 July 1609, when it was found that Robert Hylton, of Hylton, accidentally killed the young boy with a scythe. On 6 September 1609 he was to receive a free pardon. Today the ghost of the 'The Cauld Lad' lends his name to the local pub, where spirits of another sort are to be found.

English Heritage now cares for the castle at Hylton.

LANGLEY CASTLE

Overlooking the fertile valley of the South Tyne, about 1½ miles south of Hayden Bridge, stands perhaps the best example of a tower house in Northumberland: the beautiful square tower of Langley Castle. It was once a great stronghold of the de Lucys, who rebuilt the old castle that was here. In 1346, following the Battle of Crécy, Sir Thomas de Lucy was sent home to negotiate a truce with Scotland; he arrived just in time to head a column in the army that crushed the Scots at Neville's Cross. It was he, who, with the spoils of Crécy and moneys received on account of Neville's Cross, built the fortress above the Tyne. First mentioned in 1365, it was gutted by fire in 1405 on the orders of Henry IV; this was as a punishment for the revolt in the north in which Henry Percy took part. Henry was married to the Langley heiress; by 1541 it was in ruins. Sir Robert Bowes reported in 1550: 'For the most parte the fortresses towers and piles upon the utter side or frontier of those east marches have been in tymes past rased and casten downe by the Scottes and yet be not repaired which is muche pitty to see.' From the Percies it went to the Nevills, and in the seventeenth century to the Radcliffes. The prosecution of James Radcliffe, the Earl of Derwent, for his part in the Jacobite Rebellion of 1715 led to the confiscation of his property; it passed into the Trustees of Greenwich Hospital, who sold it on to the late restorer. Ruined and neglected it seemed that Langley had died, until that is, Mr Cadwallader Bates, the Northumbrian historian, bought the estate in 1882. He began to restore it to its former glory; sadly he was to die before he could complete his work. His wife Josephine d'Encharvines dedicated the chapel that is on the roof to his memory. The castle, like Haughton, is rectangular in shape with four square towers at the angles. Its appearance is little different from what it must have been when the Lucy banner blew in the breeze. Hodgson, the Northumbrian chronicler, was rather lyrical about Langley:

> While I gaze on it, even at a great distance, seems to bid a stern defiance to the attacks of time, as if determined once again to resume its roof and hang out over its battlements its blue flag and pillared canopy of morning smoke, as emblems that joy and high minded hospitality have returned to reside in it.

Six hundred years on, the fact that so much of it has survived says much for the quality of the ashlar masonry. Beneath its vaulted ground floors was the vaulted basement, which housed the kitchen and stores. The double-chamfered east entrance has a portcullis slot, and inside the roof vaulting is a boss in the form of a face, through the mouth of which the portcullis chain passed. On the west side of the castle the external arcading of the south-west turret marks the garderobes on an affluent scale. There are twelve in total – a unique series of latrines arranged above each other in three groups of four, and each recess has a pointed arch in which the stone corbels carried the seats. With this number of garderobes Langley was more than just a family residence. The entrance to the first floor hall is via a newel stair and through a double doorway.

Prior to it becoming a hotel, the castle was a private girls school whose headmistress was a Miss Hebron.

LUDWORTH TOWER

The manor house at Ludworth was once a considerable stronghold and the earliest mention to it is as being a property of the priors of Durham; the ruins of the tower are on its outskirts. It is one of the few pele towers in County Durham. From the early thirteenth century the de Ludworths, who took their name from the place, held the manor. Some 200 years later, Sir Thomas Holden was to enlarge it with a wall of stone and lime when Bishop Langley granted him a licence to fortify his manor house. Some time later it was thought necessary to rebuild the upper part of the tower and its height was raised to four storeys. The ground floor is tunnel-vaulted and above it can be seen the remains of an upper chamber which would have been lit by the embrasured window. From the Holdens it was to pass to a Roger Thornton, whose daughter married into the Lambton family of Chester-le-Street. It is sad that only a few fragments of this building now survive: the barrel-vaulted basement, the three-storey west wall and fragments of the newel stair in the south wall.

The site is managed by the City of Durham.

LUMLEY CASTLE

Lumley Castle, one of the finest castles in County Durham, stands in a park beside the River Wear. From the east it is an impressive sight; mellowed by the centuries, its battlemented walls of yellow stone rise above the steep wooded banks of Lumley Beck.

The Lumleys are one of the few families whose ancestry goes back through time to the Saxon era. From before the days of Edward the Confessor, Lumley has succeeded Lumley as lord of these estates. They were one of the first of the large families to convert from Catholicism to Protestantism.

The first Lumley of any note was Ralph, who became head of the family at the age of fourteen and was to play a key role in the defence of Berwick on Tweed in 1388. He was captured at the Battle of Otterburn and release was obtained by the payment of a large ransom, part of which was paid by Richard II. Following his release he obtained from the King and the Bishop of Durham permission 'to build anew his house at Lumley and to embattle and crenellate it with walls of stone and lime'. However, his opposition to Henry IV caused the Lumley lands to be forfeit. The lands were later returned to his son, and the Barony to his grandson, but in the reign of Henry VIII lost once again with the beheading of George Lumley on the charge of High Treason – he had taken part in the 'Rising of the North'. Together with his wife Jane he was taken to London where he was hung, drawn and quartered. His head and 'quarters' were then stuck on to pikes and displayed above the gates of London. Jane, his wife, was burned like a witch, as Henry deemed it degrading for a lady to be quartered in front of the vulgar crowd. His son John Lumley, who was also a rebel, succeeded in keeping his head on his shoulders, as well as his lands, by making his peace with Queen Elizabeth. John was to make considerable alterations to the castle he loved, and he is also responsible for the fourteen effigies that line the north wall in the church of St Mary's at Chester-le-Street. They were placed here in 1594 and are known locally as Lumley's warriors. The historian Camden was to describe him as 'a man most honourable for all the ornament of true nobility'. His grandson Richard made other changes early in the eighteenth century when he employed the great John Vanbrugh. Richard was by now the 1st Earl of Scarborough, and had been one of the leading Royalist officers at the Battle of Sedgemoor. Sedgemoor will be remembered for the infamous Judge Jeffries trials. So ferocious were his judgements that he became known as the Hanging Judge and his court the Bloody Assizes.

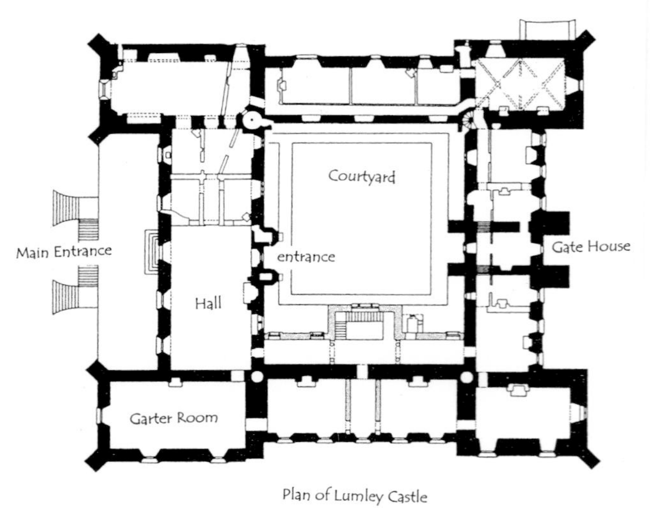

Plan of Lumley Castle

Lumley stands foursquare, with a battlemented tower at each corner, often referred to as a Tower House. Castles such as this were built with the domestic comfort of its owner in mind. The approach to the castle is from the west, up a tree-lined avenue, and the towers on this western side are as commanding as they are on the east. At each corner octagonal turrets surmount the buttresses of the towers. The east front, overlooking Lumley Beck, retains many of its medieval features, and it is here that one finds the original entrance. Passing through the gatehouse leads one to the quadrangle, where a stone lined well can be seen in one corner. On the west side of the quadrangle, flanked by semi-octagonal turrets, is the original entrance to the Great Hall. Above its low entrance a series of heraldic shields are to be seen, the topmost of which is that of Richard II, who was king at the time the castle was built. It also bears the arms of France, for Richard claimed the French crown through his great-grandmother who was the heiress of France. The Great Hall on the first floor is said to be the finest room of the castle. Vanbrugh altered little, apart from the windows. The ornate fireplace was built in Tudor times, upon its over-mantel the arms and motto of the Lumleys. A broad plaited design known as a guilloche crosses the fireplace between two Roman Doric columns. The solar was on the first floor of the south-west tower adjoining the hall, a room that has since been known as the Banqueting Hall and the Ballroom and is now called the Garter Room, from the Star of that Order that forms part of the plaster stucco of the ceiling. This is generally believed to be the work of Pietro Francini in 1740. The walls are also in plaster, with the cameos of past Roman emperors made by the Italian workmen brought here by the 3rd Earl of Scarborough. Vanbrugh was to transform the undercroft below the Garter Room into a library. With its three-groin vaulted aisles, stone fireplace and rusticated piers it seems to be more an imitation of his style. The castle, like many others, has its ghost. Lady Lumley, the wife of Ralph, is said to wander the corridors at night searching for her husband. She was murdered by priests and her body thrown into the castle's well.

Six hundred years on the castle is still in the hands of the Lumleys; however, it is now leased as a luxury hotel. As it stands today, with its picturesque flight of steps leading up to its front entrance, it has an air of defiant quietness, and all recollection of past wars has left its tranquil façade.

MORTHAM TOWER

Although tower houses are rare in Durham, they do appear like lone sentinels standing at the fringe of reiver country. Mortham Tower, standing close to Barnard Castle (see page 91), is the most southerly of these. Repeatedly attacked by the Scots, the tower was to protect the village; local records show that it had been quite large with a small number of prosperous families living there. However, the Scots destroyed the hamlet of Mortham together with its church during a raid in 1346. Only the pele and a few gravestones survived. Some time later the gravestones were to be used in the buttresses of the gate that leads to the courtyard. In his stay at Rokeby Sir Walter Scott had this to say of the tower: 'The battlements of the tower are singularly elegant, the architect having broken them at regular intervals into different heights; while those at the corners of the tower project into octagonal turrets.'

The building is a fortified manor house with hall, solar, and north-west wing built in the reign of Henry VII. The solar was remodelled as the Great Chamber at the end of the sixteenth century, while the hall was altered to a barn around 1820. Most of the windows are square-headed, with mullions and hood-moulds, which are chamfered and have hollow-chamfered surrounds. The first floor Great Chamber has richly-moulded ceiling beams as well as a Tudor-arched fireplace. In the tower itself there are other old fireplaces, garderobes and windows that have stone seats. The central gateway, which is built in to the south courtyard wall, has double-chamfered arch and a hollow chamfered hood mould. The fifteenth-century restorations were by the Rokeby family, who strengthened the tower before they took up residence. The family arms of three rooks appear on an outer wall; and at the end of the house is a barmkin that was used for the protection of their cattle.

PRUDHOE CASTLE

Perched on a prominent spur that overlooks the River Tyne stands the castle of Prudhoe. It was built in 1165 by Odinel de Umfraville on the site of a motte and bailey to guard a strategic crossing on the River Tyne. Robin with the Beard was the first of the Umfravilles to arrive in England, and for his services William the Conqueror granted him the Barony of Redesdale. William was then to grant the Barony of Prudhoe to the Umfravilles. The first mention of the castle is in 1173 when it came under siege from William the Lion of Scotland following his laying claim to the Earldom of Northumberland. He was furious at Odinel, with whom he had been brought up, for his refusal to join him, and declared he would be cursed and excommunicated rather than grant terms to Prudhoe. The following year the castle again was to come under siege. In their frustration his followers destroyed the gardens and cornfields outside the castle walls and stripped the bark from the trees in the orchard. After three days he was forced to retreat to Alnwick where he was taken prisoner by Bernard de Baliol. The last of the Umfravilles was Gilbert, who died in 1381. His widow, the Countess Maud, then became the wife of Henry Percy, 4th Lord of Alnwick. It was through this marriage that Prudhoe passed into the hands of the Percies. They were to lose Prudhoe and their all estates for their part in the rebellion against Henry IV but Queen Mary restored these in 1557; they have retained them to the present day.

When approaching the castle from the south one crosses the dam, which is on the side of the millpond. To the right are the ruins of the castle mill. A long narrow barbican, which dates from the fourteenth century, leads through to the gatehouse and into the outer bailey. The barbican was without any portcullis, but had iron lattice gates at each end of its passageway. This is tunnel-vaulted with a transverse arch resting on a pair of head corbels. In the thirteenth century a small chapel was built above the gatehouse, and the sanctuary is corbelled out with three lancet-shaped lights; this is the earliest known oriel window to be seen in England. The impressive keep, with its tall turret rising above the rest of the castle, stands in the west ward and is one of the smallest Norman keeps in England and, apart from Norham, the oldest in Northumberland. A newel stair ascends from the basement to the first floor, and then in the thickness of the walls towards the roof. The massive curtain wall of the outer bailey is well preserved and contains a fine example of a garderobe. As for the other buildings that stood in the bailey none have survived; the Great Hall and its kitchens, the bakehouse and the brewery – all have gone.

It was near here, on Monday 28 January 1766, that a certain William Fenwick and his friends were foxhunting. After some hours of chase the fox sought its safety in the nearby drift of a coalmine; in darkness and hot pursuit the hounds followed for almost an hour. Finally they caught up with the fox and killed it before it could reach daylight and escape.

RABY CASTLE

Raby Castle, with its great long battlemented front and its protective walls, readily conforms to the image that we have of a medieval castle. Situated in pleasant parkland about a mile to the north of the village of Staindrop, it is one of the finest castles in England. The first known mention that we have of Raby was in the reign of King Canute, when he was Emperor of the North. Then merely a small estate, he was to give it to St Cuthbert as a deed of gift after his barefoot pilgrimage from Garmondsway near Trimdon. It is not known if this referred only to the land, for there is no mention of a building. The castle came into the possession of the Nevills through Isabella de Nevill, an heiress, when she married one Robert de FitzMaldred lord of Raby. It was Bishop Hatfield who granted to the 3rd Earl, John de Nevill, the licence to crenellate his manor in the May of 1378. In it, Bishop Hatfield writes

> . . . that he may of his Manor of Raby,
> which is within the bishopric of Durham,
> make a castle freely at his own will,
> and may embattle and crenellate all the
> towers, houses and walls thereof, without
> being hindered, molested, grieved or
> disturbed by us or any of our officers,
> ministers or other subjects, dwelling
> within our said royal seigniory.

A free hand: such were the powers of the Prince bishops in the palatine, where 'the King's writ runneth not'. The days that were to become significant to Raby are from the time of Ralph Nevill, the hero of Neville's Cross and his son, John; some time High Admiral of England.

It was to remain the family stronghold until the eleventh year of the reign of Elizabeth I, the year 1569. On 13 November, Charles, 6th Earl of Northumberland, assembled 700 knights in the Great Barons' Hall to plot the disastrous 'Rising of the North' with the intention to replace Mary, Queen of Scots on the throne. This enterprise brought about the demise of the house of Nevill. Defeated he escaped abroad to lead a beggarly existence and Raby was forfeit to the Crown. After the 'Rising in the North' the Raby estates returned to the crown

James I granted that they were to provide revenues for his son Charles. One of the trustees, Sir Henry Vane, had advanced money to the young prince and applied to the King that he could keep Raby in exchange. It is still in the possession of this family today. Only once have the castle walls been breached, and that was by the English during the Civil War. Sir Henry Vane was principal Secretary of State to Charles I, but afterwards he was led to support the Parliament which led to Raby being besieged by royal forces. In 1741 the first Lord Barnard, angered by his son's marriage, sold the entire contents of the castle, cut down the trees and attempted to destroy the castle; but following legal action he was ordered to break off and make good the damage.

Tradition has it that a hearth fire has burned in this castle since the time of Edward the Confessor. An underground passage, now blocked off, led from the cellars through to Staindrop Abbey.

A visit to Raby can be an evocative experience. The drive winds through the park until it reaches the castle's impressive gatehouse with its portcullis grooves. Once through the gatehouse, which at one time was guarded by a drawbridge, the visitor finds himself within an area that was enclosed by the moat. Here a low curtain wall about 3 feet high runs from the gatehouse to enclose the castle; soaring above are its impregnable towers. No two are equal in height or shape – from Clifford's Tower at 80 feet to Joan's Tower at 61 feet, with the Bulmer's Tower, Chapel Tower, the keep, Kitchen Tower, Nevill Tower, Raskelf and Watch somewhere between the two. The Clifford Tower, behind the gatehouse, with walls that are 10 feet thick in places, still retains some of its original windows. To the left of it, in front of the inner keep, lies the Kitchen Tower. It contains the fourteenth-century kitchen that was used for more than 600 years. An unusual feature here is a passage in the thickness of the wall that linked the five windows used by archers in times of emergency. Moving on we have the Raskelf Tower named after one of the Nevill manors in Yorkshire, with four turrets on its roof and a low wall to the front. Beyond is the Chapel

Tower and five-sided Bulmer's named after a Norman knight. This is thought to be the oldest part of the castle. Joan's Tower is named after John of Gaunt's daughter, who married the 6th Baron of Raby, Ralph Nevill. It was their daughter, Lady Cecily Nevill, who was to become known as the Rose of Raby. She was to suffer at the hands of her son the Duke of Clarence when at his trial he accused her of adultery. He stated that the late King's true father had been an archer named Blackburn, and that she also had an adulterous affair with Miles Forest, Keeper of the Wardrobe. Forest was to make a deathbed confession as to his part in the murder of the two Princes in the Tower. In the spring of 1486, the *Croyland Chronicle* was to write: 'A rumour was spread that the sons of King Edward had died a violent death, but it was uncertain how'. Dominic Mancini, who left England in July 1483 had this to say:

> He and his brother were withdrawn into the inner apartments of the Tower proper, and day by day began to be seen more rarely behind the bars and windows, till at length they ceased to appear altogether. A Strasbourg doctor, the last of his attendants, whose services the King enjoyed, reported that the young King, like a victim prepared for sacrifice, sought remission of his sins by daily confession and penance, because he believed that death was facing him. Already there was a suspicion that he had been done away with.

Set right inside the castle on the north side of the courtyard is the Entrance Hall, with a carriage drive straight through it to allow guests to alight at the foot of the staircase. Like all castles it has its ghosts, and Raby has three. First we have the spectre of Charles Nevill stalking the Barons' Hall, where he plotted the Rising of the North. Then we have the headless figure of Henry Vane the Younger, who roams through the library. And finally the First Lady Barnard, known as the Old Hell Cat, who, seething over the memory of her son's wedding that she disapproved of, wanders the ramparts at night knitting with red-hot needles.

WITTON CASTLE, BISHOP AUCKLAND

Standing on the south bank of the River Wear a few miles upstream from Bishop Auckland is Witton Castle. The manor here is thought to have been that of the old manor of Wichtun; recorded as having been granted to Henry de Pudsey by Henry II in the latter part of the twelfth century. Henry was the son of Hugh de Pudsey, the Bishop of Durham. Unlike many of the castles in Northumberland, Witton was never an ancestral home of any one family for very long. The longest tenure is that of the Eure family who aquired the lands in the fourteenth century. Early in the fifteenth century Bishop Langley discovered that Ralph de Eure had begun to fortify his manor house without applying for a licence; he was to be later pardoned for this infringement and allowed to 'inclose his manor, with a wall of lime and stone'. The very fact that work had commenced before the requisite licence had been granted caused the historian William Fordyce to write 'none but such as supposed themselves to be almost above the law would have acted in such a manner'. The main features of the castle are the keep, the two fortified gateways in the curtain wall and the three angle towers. The courtyard is quite large and was used by tenants of the manor during the Border wars as a refuge. In the curtain wall we have an unusual feature. Iron shutters in the crenellations protected the high parapet of the broad sentry walk; these shutters were pivoted and could be swung into place in times of danger. The keep is oblong in plan lying east to west and, like the bartizans, projects beyond the curtain wall at the north side of the bailey. It also has a barrel-vaulted basement, and a newal stair ascends from there to what was the Great Hall on the first floor. High on the exterior of the curtain wall are rows of round holes; these were to take the supports for the brattices from which the walls could be better defended. The bartizans too had their brattices; projecting angles were a weak spot in any wall and this explains their placing and purpose. Only three of the four now remain; the one at the north-west was destroyed with part of the curtain wall in the eighteen-century when buildings were added to the keep. Standing at the south-west corner of the bailey is the square bartizan. There is a guardroom here, with entrances from the battlements on both sides. The south-east bartizan is corbelled out from the curtain wall and contains a small guardroom. Its roof can be reached by means of a stairway corbelled out from the curtain wall. The rain gutters end in a series of carved human heads round its outer face.

In 1963 the Witton estates came up for sale and was bought by Lord Lambton; the famous 'Red Boy' portrait by Sir Thomas Lawrence that used to be at Witton is now in Lord Lambton's London home.

WILLIMOTESWYKE CASTLE

This strangely named castle is in an out-of-the-way location. It lies on a back road through Ridley and Beltingham, on the south side of the river, close to Bardon Mill. The first mention of it is in the survey of 1541, and it was noted as belonging to one Nicholas Ridley and having a 'good tower and stone house'. This to is the birthplace of Bishop Ridley who burned at the stake at Balliol College Oxford in 1555. His martyrdom is said to have 'lit a candle' for the Protestant cause. He and Bishop Latimer were responsible for forcing Edward VI against his will to order the burning of Joan of Kent.

In the manner of the day a bill was submitted to the Government for the burning.

For three loads of wood faggots for burning Ridley and Latimer	12s 0d
Item, one load of furze faggots	3s 4d
For the carriage of these loads	2s 0d
Item: a post	1s 4d
Two chains	3s 4d
Two staples	6d
Four labourers	2s 8d
Total	£1 5s 2d

Not long before the Bishop's martyrdom the Ridleys were involved with the Thirlwalls in the murder of Sir Albany Featherstonehaugh, a neighbour with whom they had a feud. Scott describes the raid on Featherstonehaugh in the first canto of his poem 'Marmion'.

How the fierce Thirwalls and Ridleys all,
Stout Willimoteswick,
And that Hard riding Dick,
And Hughie of Hawden and Will o' the wal
Have set on Sir Albany Featherstonehaugh,
And taken his life at the Deadmanshaw.

The gatehouse is of the Dunstanburgh type, although, of course, on a smaller scale, having a gatehouse and barmkin. The entrance is tunnel vaulted with the top storey corbelled out on three projected roll mouldings. On the corbelling some of the waterspouts have the appearance of guns. In the courtyard the manor house has had to put up with many alterations across its five hundred years; but the great fireplace managed to escape these and is still in its place.

It is interesting to note that some 400-odd years ago, when the owner was one Nicholas Ridley, grandnephew to Bishop Ridley, an inventory was made of its contents; it recorded that in the sitting room were the following goods: twenty pairs of double linen sheets, ten pairs of 'strakinge' sheets, ten pairs of 'harne' sheets, six 'wishons', six 'worset wishons', six candlesticks, a new cupboard, a 'hurle bed', a new 'presser', seven chests, two 'carping' cloths, two cupboard cloths, four new sacks, the 'Boke of Marters' and a Bible.

But their support of Charles I during the Civil War in 1642 ensured that their lands were forfeit. No more would the Ridleys ride out on some dubious venture.

This is a now a Scheduled Monument protected by law.

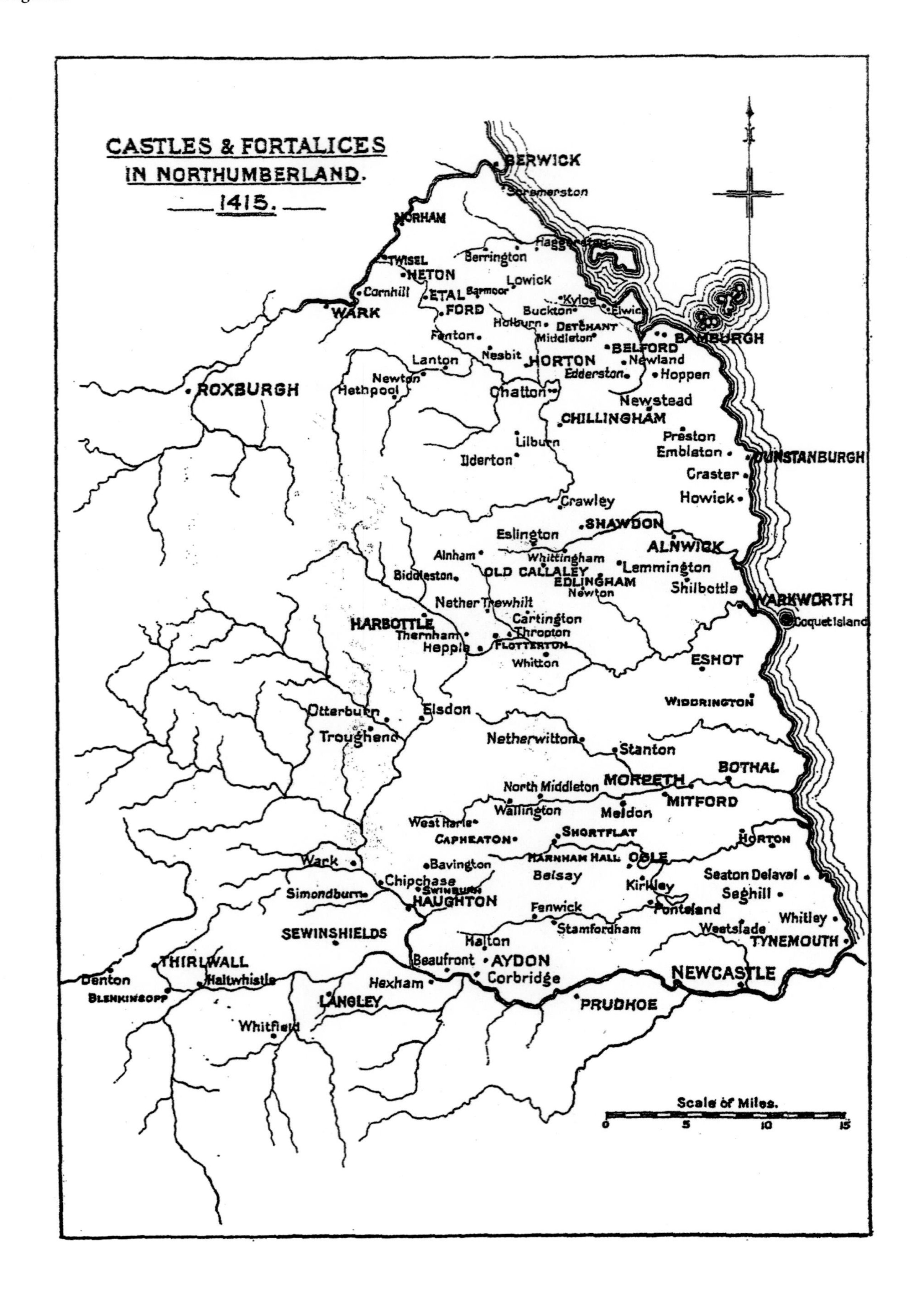
CASTLES & FORTALICES
IN NORTHUMBERLAND.
1415.
BERWICK
NORHAM
TWISEL
HETON
Cornhill
ETAL
FORD
WARK
Berrington
Lowick
Barmoor
Kyloe
Buckton
Elwick
DETCHANT
Middleton
BAMBURGH
BELFORD
Newland
Hoppen
Fenton
Nesbit
Lanton
HORTON
Edderston
Newton
Hethpool
ROXBURGH
Chatton
Newstead
CHILLINGHAM
Preston
Embleton
DUNSTANBURGH
Lilburn
Ilderton
Craster
Howick
Crawley
SHAWDON
Eslington
ALNWICK
Alnham
Whittingham
Lemmington
Biddleston
OLD CALLALEY
EDLINGHAM
Newton
Shilbottle
WARKWORTH
Coquet Island
Nether Trewhitt
Cartington
HARBOTTLE
Thropton
Hepple
Whitton
ESHOT
WIDDRINGTON
Otterburn
Elsdon
Troughend
Netherwitton
Stanton
BOTHAL
North Middleton
MORPETH
MITFORD
Wallington
Meldon
West Harle
CAPHEATON
SHORTFLAT
HORTON
HARNHAM HALL
OGLE
Wark
Bavington
Belsay
Kirkley
Seaton Delaval
Seghill
Chipchase
Simondburn
SWINBURN
HAUGHTON
Fenwick
Ponteland
Whitley
Stamfordham
Westslade
TYNEMOUTH
SEWINSHIELDS
Halton
THIRLWALL
Beaufront
AYDON
Corbridge
NEWCASTLE
Denton
Haltwhistle
Hexham
BLENKINSOPP
LANGLEY
PRUDHOE
Whitfield
Scale of Miles.
0
5
10
15

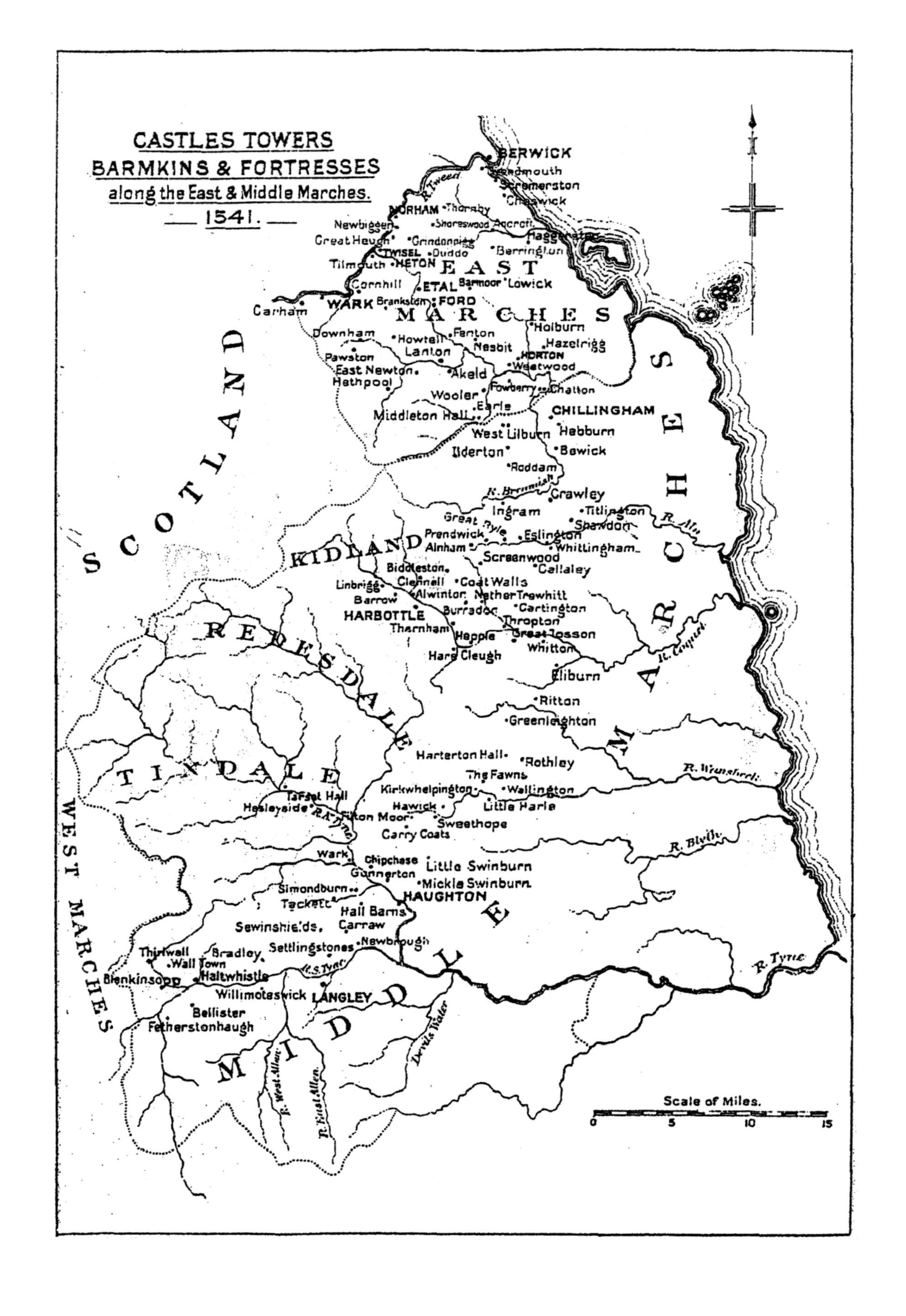
CASTLES TOWERS
BARMKINS & FORTRESSES
along the East & Middle Marches.
1541.
SCOTLAND
EAST MARCHES
MIDDLE MARCHES
KIDLAND
REDESDALE
TINDALE
WEST MARCHES
BERWICK
NORHAM
CHILLINGHAM
HARBOTTLE
HAUGHTON
LANGLEY
Scale of Miles.
0 5 10 15

OTHER FORTIFIED SITES

Alwinton Bastle: *Location NT 892 062*
The vicar at Alwinton, like so many of the Border clergy, lived in a fortified house in the Middle Ages. The 1541 survey tells us: 'At Allaynton ys a lytle bastell house of stone, the mansion of the vycaredge scarely in good rep'ac'ons.' In the seventeenth century it came into the possession of John Heron, who let it as an alehouse; the vicar then had to build himself a small cottage. It later fell into decay and the site is no longer known.

Beafront Castle: *Location NY 963 659*
Today nothing survives of the castle of Beafront, first mentioned in the survey of 1415. In the reign of Elizabeth I it was the residence of the Carnaby family; later it was to come into the possession of the Errington family who built a large mansion on the site. In 1836 Dobson was to transform this into a grand country house.

Berrington Tower: *Location NU007 432*
The first record of it as a tower was in 1415 but by 1541 it was in ruins. On their survey The Border Commissioners had this to report: 'At Berryngton beynge thre myles from the said ryver of Twede there was a towre of thinheritance of therle of Rutland which for lacke of reparacons ys lately fallen to extreme ruyne & decaye.' There are no traces to be seen here today.

Biddlestone Tower: *Location NT 955 083*
The tower at Biddlestone is still to be seen, albeit as a chapel. The Hall which stood here was said to have been the model for 'Osbaldistone Hall' in *Rob Roy* by Sir Walter Scott; and the Selbys who owned it were Catholics and would fit the story. Mentioned in the 1415 and 1541 surveys, the remains of the tower were to become the foundations on which the Selby's built their family chapel at the beginning of the nineteenth century. The vaulted basement of the tower now forms the undercroft of the chapel.

Brankston Tower: *Location NT 893 375*
Brankston is now famous in British history as being the scene of the battle of Flodden. It is first mentioned in 1541 as a 'lytle towyre without a barmkin' that was destroyed several times by the Scots. Although there is documentary evidence of this pele no evidence remains on the ground.

Burradon Tower: *Location NZ 277 730*
Standing midway between Newcastle and Blyth, in the grounds of a nineteenth-century farmhouse and in sight of the sea, is the ruined pele of Burradon. The stonework is of rough rubble with large well-cut quoins and at roof level the remains of a parapet carried on corbels can be seen. There are machicolations over the entrance and the vaulted basement has a newal stair.

Capheaton Castle: *Location NZ 059 817*
The tower recorded in the 1415 list had both moat and drawbridge. It was incorporated into a house sometime in the sixteenth century, and this was altered and extended in the eighteenth century. The tower adjoins the left side of the house of which has walls of a similar thickness to the tower; this would suggest that at one time there might have been two towers linked by a central hall.

Chatton Tower: *Location NU 039 293*
In the 1415 survey there were two towers at Chatton, the vicar's pele and Fowberyes Tower. Fowberyes, an oblong tower house that was rebuilt in 1666, was capable of holding a garrison of eighty men. A nineteenth-century vicarage now stands on the site of the vicar's pele and there are no signs of an earlier tower.

Crawley Tower: *Location NU 068 165*
High above the Breamish at the east corner of a Roman camp stands Crawley tower. Now surrounded by farm buildings there is little left to show what the tower looked like when it was licensed to crenellate in 1343. It was reported to have fallen into decay at the 1541 survey.

Eshot Castle: *Location NZ 201 906*
Little remains of the castle mentioned in the survey of 1415. Permission to crenellate was first given in 1310 to Sir Roger de Mauduit when he fortified his manor house. The site is on low-lying ground near to two streams.

Fawns Castle: *Location NZ 007 853*
The Fawnes is first mention in a document written in 1303 as a square enclosure surrounded by a moat. In 1541 Sir Robert Bowes reported: 'At the Sawnes is a lytle Pele house or bastell in thinherytaunce of the said John Fenwyke in measurable good rep'ac'ons'. This appears to be the only reference to this pele tower.

Fenton Tower: *Location NZ 963 335*
The tower, built with a barmkin, appears on both the 1415 and 1541 lists. Said to be in a state of disrepair in 1541 it was abandoned in 1603 and later dismantled. At one time it accommodated 100 foot soldiers under Sir John Forster.

Fenwick Tower: *Location NZ 057 729*
Of the tower at Maften that John de Fenwick was licensed to crenellate in 1378 little remains. In 1775, when part of the tower was being taken down, a box containing over 200 gold coins dating from the reigns of Edward III and Richard II was found beneath its vaulted floor. It is believed that it was part of a ransom for Sir John Fenwick's two sons, who were being held prisoners by the Scots.

Harnham Hall: *Location NZ073 804*
Directly above an outcrop of rock a short distance from Belsay is the site of Harnham Hall. Originally a part of the barony of Bolam the present Hall includes part of the old fifteenth-century tower of the Swinburnes, which stood here in earlier times. In 1667 the estate passed into the hands of Major Babington, the Governor of Berwick. The Hall was listed in the 1415 list of castles as a 'turris'.

Hazelrigg Tower: *Location NU 056 331*
Hazelrigg, 3 miles west of Belford, was in the barony of Alnwick. The tower here, first mentioned in 1514, was capable of holding a garrison of twenty men. Sir Robert Bowes survey of 1541 tells us, 'At Hesellerygge ys a lowe towre which was never fully fynyshed of thinherytaunce of Thomas Haggarstone esquier kepte in measurable good rep'acons'.

Hepple Tower: *Location NT 986 006*
Hepple Tower is first mentioned in the 1415 Border survey as being held by Sir Robert Ogle, who also had six other buildings listed. In 1509 twenty men garrisoned it, but at the time of the 1541 survey it had fallen into decay. The remains of the tower today indicate that it was a much longer building with a barrel-vaulted ground floor. A newel stair set into the thickness of the wall at one time led to the upper floors.

Hetton Castle: *Location NT 901 419*
In 1415 Hetton castle was in the possession of Sir Thomas Grey. A plan of it in the reign of Elizabeth I shows a number of buildings in a quadrangle enclosure with four corner towers and curtain walls. It was destroyed by James IV in 1496. Considered suitable for restoration the report of the Commissioners on the Borders in 1584 read 'This castle or fortresse we doe thincke a verye fit and convenient place to defend the countrye and annoye the enemye as aforesaid if it were repaired the charges of which reparacions we esteeme as it hath bene to fyve hundreth thre score pounde or to thre hundreth pounde to make it sufficient for a garrison of horsemen' (£560 to restore: £300 for 50 horsemen). The site today is covered by farm buildings.

Holburn Tower: *Location NU 04 06*
The monks of Lindisfarne built the tower some time between 1350 and 1415, when it first appeared in the survey. It was said to be suitable for the garrisoning of twenty men after being reconditioned with a barmkin in 1541. It was abandoned shortly after.

Hoppen Tower: *Location NU 161 306*
A 'Turris de Hopyn' is listed in the survey of 1415; no sign of the building survives and its exact whereabouts is uncertain.

Horton Castle, Blyth: *Location NZ 280 796*
It was in 1292 that Sir Guischard de Charron was given a licence to crenellate his manor house at Horton and a few fragments of it survive in the farm buildings at West Horton. Later it was to come into the possession of the Delaval family, who dismantled it in the nineteenth century. The course of a moat can still be traced.

Horton Castle, Chatton: *Location NU 027 308*
Sir Robert Bowes, in his report of 1541 tells us 'At Horton there is a greatt towre with a barmekin of Sir Roger Grayes Inherytaunce and his chiefe house in great decay for lack of contynuall rep'ac'ons'. First mentioned in the survey of 1415 as a 'Great Tower' it fell into decay in the sixteenth century. It was rebuilt as a house in the seventeenth century but once more fell into ruin and was demolished in the nineteenth century. Nothing remains of the site today.

Ilderton Tower: *Location NU 016 217*
The tower with barmkin had fallen into a ruinous state by 1541 and was said to be capable of garrisoning fifty men if repaired. It is believed to have been incorporated into the building of Ilderton Hall.

Kyloe Tower: *Location NU 059 397*
The remains of the tower listed in 1451 now forms part of farm buildings at East Kyloe. Corbels in the vaulted basement indicate there was a loft in the roof as at Hepple. Access to the upper floor was by means of a newel stair. In 1541 it was held by David Grey and had a barmkin with low walls.

Lilburn Tower: *Location NU 021 242*
Set in the grounds of Lilburn Tower is the ruins of West Lilburn Tower. In the survey of 1541 there were two towers here, one belonging to Cuthbert Proctor, which had fallen into decay and one belonging to Sir Cuthbert Ogle, which had suffered from a fire. It was suggested that they be both restored so that in times of war they could house one hundred men.

Nafferton Castle: *Location NZ 073 658*
North of Prudhoe, off the A69, are the remains of Nafferton Castle. It was built without a licence, which resulted in it being dismantled; it is marked as Lonkin's Hall on old O.S. maps and associated with the ballad that grew up around it.

Nesbit Tower: *Location NT 984 336*
In 1415 the tower here belonged to Sir Thomas Grey; but by 1541 Sir Robert Bowes was to report 'At Nesbit there was a towre of thinherytaunce of Sir Roger Graye but yt is longe synce for lack of reparacons decayed and fallen and no fortresse there nowe remayneth.'

Netherwitton Castle: *Location NZ 102 904*
The castle at Witton built by Roger de Thornton was incorporated into a country house for Sir Nicholas Thornton in the seventeenth century. In the survey of 1415 it was described as 'Turris de Witton iuxta aquam'. Cromwell was to stay here in 1651 when on his way to Scotland.

Newland Tower: *Location NU116 324*
A licence to crenellate was granted to Sir John de Middleton in 1310 and though it is listed in the 1415 survey no trace of the site can be seen.

Ogle Castle: *Location NZ 141 791*
What little remained of Ogle Castle was incorporated in the manor house that stands on the left bank of Ogle Burn. It was in 1341 that Sir Robert de Ogle was licensed to crenellate his manor house at Ogle and it was here that the captured King David was brought after his defeat at Neville's Cross in 1346. A plan of 1632 shows the castle as having ranges of three sides of a courtyard.

Roddam Tower: *Location NU 025 204*
The tower listed in the 1541 survey has now vanished. The report by the Commissioners said, 'At Roddome there is a lytle toure without a barmekyn of thinherytaunce of John Roddom esquier the rooffe ys decayed for lacke of necessarye repacon'ns.' It is thought to have stood on Castle Hill overlooking Roddam Burn but no trance remains of any fortification. Armstrong shows the site on his map of the area in 1769.

Scramerston Tower: *Location NU 006 498*
Site of a pele tower with barmkin and listed in both surveys. The 1541 survey tells us that 'At Scrymmerstone upon the sea coste a myle from the said river of Twede ys a great olde towre muche for lacke of contynuall necessary reparacons and yt is of thinherytaunce of a gentlewoman that is heyre to John Swynowe and maryed to one Edmund Lawson.' There is no trace of the tower today.

Seaton Delaval Tower: *Location NZ321 765*
Sir William de Wychester held the 'Turris de seton de la vale' in 1415. Little is known about it other than it was probably demolished by Vanbrugh when landscaping the gardens for the hall. Some information can be gleaned from the Delaval records; an inventory of 1606 lists goods and chattels in the great bedchamber, the parlour and the kitchen.

Seghill Tower: *Location NZ 283 742*
Believed to have been three storeys high the tower at Seghill is listed in the survey of 1415. Within the ground floor of the now demolished old Blake Arms Hotel was the vaulted basement.

Sewingshields Tower: *Location NY 817 706*
A ploughed-out ditch are all that indicate the site of a tower held in 1415 by Sir Robert Ogle. It is recorded in the 1541 survey, as, 'At sewynsheallles is an old towre of thinherytaunce of John Chypchase esquire in great decaye in the roofe and flores and lyeth waste and unplenyshed.'

Shawdon Tower: *Location NU 092 143*
First mentioned in 1403 as being a 'Tower at Shawdon' it was listed in the survey of 1415 as the 'Castle of Shawden'. It was probably built by the Lilburns who aquired the manor in 1303. Described to be in 'measurable good repair' in 1541 it was demolished in the eighteenth century.

Shorewood Tower: *Location NT 958 466*
Shorewood stood about 2 miles south-west of Berwick. It was destroyed by James IV in 1496 when he was a supporter of Perkin Warbeck. In the Border survey of 1584 the Commissioners reported 'This towne or fortresse we do thincke a verye fitte and convenient place as well to defend the countrye as annoye the enemye upon the opposite border if it were repared the charges of which reparacions we esteem to two hundreth and fortye pounds.' Today there is nothing to be seen.

Shortflatt Tower: *Location NZ 079 811*
Like Harnham, Shortflatt Tower was part of the barony of Bolam. In the latter part of the thirteenth century it came into the possession of Robert de Raymes who also held Aydon Castle. On 5 April 1305 he was granted licence to crenellate here and at Aydon as part of his defences against the Scots. The present building, which is attached to the earlier seventeenth-century house, retains many features of its period.

Simmonburn Castle: *Location NY 862 738*
Simmonburn Tower was situated on a ridge north-west of the village. It was recommended as a post for the Keeper of Tynedale with a garrison of fifty men in 1537. The castle appears to have been a tower house with corbelled out angle turrets. Recorded in the 1541 list as a tower four storeys high and in good repair it was later abandoned by the Herons in favour of Chipchase.

Stanton Tower: *Location NZ131 895*
The building at Stanton bears little resemblance to the tower, which was occupied by John Corbet in the time of Henry VI. Over the years it has had a chequered history, being a shop, a workhouse and a blacksmiths. The oldest part of the building is the remains of a pele, which is oblong having a south projection.

Staward Pele: *Location NY 800 607*
Staward Pele is the most secluded of all Northumberland's towers. No castle in the county is better placed. It stands on a steep promontory on the confluence of two rivers: the Allen and Harsingdale Burn. In 1386 the Duke of York gave the pele to the Eremite Friars of Hexham for an annual payment of five marks. Staward belonged to that group of Northumbrian strongholds which consisted of curtain and gatehouse only; of these Dunstanburgh is the best example.

Tarset Castle: *Location NY 788 854*
Tarset Castle occupied a strong position on the left bank of Tarset Burn. The earliest known example to crenellate is that granted by Henry III to John Cumyn in 1267 when he was given permission to fortify his manor at 'Tyrset'. Leland, who came to Northumberland in 1538, tells us that the castle at Tarset was in ruins. The grassy mounds of masonry that survive hold little of interest to the antiquary.

Thropton Tower: *Location NU 026 023*
Sir Edward Radcliffe was garrisoned here in 1509 with sixteen men. Today there is no sign of the tower that is in the list of 1541.

Titlington Tower: *Location NU 098 150*
Titlington Tower is believed to have been built on the ruins of a motte and bailey. The tower belonged the Crown when Sir Robert Bowes made his survey in 1541; it is believed that the tower was incorporated into a house in the mid-eighteenth century.

Troughend Tower: *Location NY 866 924*
A medieval document refers to a tower held by the de Butycombe family at 'Trowhen' in 1415. Although it appears on the 1415 list there is nothing visible of the site today.

Wark Castle: *Location NY 861 768*
Wark was once the capital of Tynedale and traces of motte and bailey can be found here on Moat Hill. It is believed to have been built by prince Henry of Scotland, after he was created Earl of Northumberland in 1139. In 1415 it was listed as being the property of Sir Thomas Grey.

West Lilburn Tower: *Location NU 021 241*
The parish of Lilburn lies on the edge of the Cheviots and the ruins of West Lilburn Tower is situated on a spur of land above the valley. It belonged to the Lilburns and Clennells who had there seats here in the reign of Edward II.

Whitfield Tower: *Location NY 778 564*
The tower, first mentioned in the list of 1415 as belonging to Mathew Whitfield, lies in the village of Whitfield 5 miles west of Allendale. It was razed to the ground in 1785 and the stonework used to build Whitfield Hall.

Whitley Castle: *Location N357 958*
In 1345 Gilbert de Whitley received his licence to fortify his manor house from King Edward III. The tower that he built passed, through the marriage of his daughter, to William Parker in 1356. Listed in the 1415 survey as a 'turris' it was destroyed shortly before the survey of 1541.

Widdrington Castle: *Location NZ 155 958*
The 1415 survey has this site recorded as a 'castle or tower of Wodryngton' and belonging to the de Widdringtons. James VI of Scotland stayed here on his way to claim the English throne in 1603. In 1720 it was said to be 'in danger of falling and inhabitable save only for a small part'. It was destroyed by fire in 1862 and only a mound 7 feet high survives today.

Wooler Tower: *Location NT 992 280*
The early castle at Wooler fell into ruin because of the absent owners. It was in the possession of Odinel Ford when it was recorded as 'a certain waste-fortress and not of any value'. The high mound on which the remains stand dominates the town. Its strategic importance was recognised by Sir Robert Bowes in his survey of 1541 when he strongly urged its repair. His advice does not seem to have been acted upon as the castle was soon in ruins. Little is known of the part it played in the history of the Borders.

GLOSSARY

abutment Meeting of an arch or vault with its support.
achitectural styles
Saxon: before the Nornam Conquest
Norman: eleventh and twelfth centuries
Gothic: end of thirteenth century
aisle The space alongside the nave or transept of a church
arbalest A crossbow; a medieval French corruption from the Latin word 'arcuballista'.
arcade A series of arches supported by columns.
ashlar Masonery of large blocks wrought to even faces and square edges.
attic A top storey of a building.
bailey Courtyard area around the motte or keep of a castle.
barbican The outwork defending the entrance to a castle
barmkin The enclosure of pele and bastle houses.
barrel vaulted Arched over like a tunnel in one direction.
barrow Burial mound.
bartizan A parapet or projecting gallery often applied to a corbelled corner turret; square or round.
bastion A projecting structure at a corner of a fortification.
battlement Fortified parapet, designed so that archers could shoot through the crenellations.
belfry Bell tower or chamber where the bells are hung.
billhook A long shaft with a hook for unhorsing knights.
bracket A small projecting piece of stone to support a horizontal member.
brattice A covered wooden gallery on a castle for defence.
Bronze Age The period in Britain from 2000 to 600 BC.
buttress Support built against a wall to stabilise it. There are four types: clasping, setback, diagonal and angle.
cairn A mound of stones; usually covering a burial mound.
castellated Battlemented.
cinquefoil Ornamental window with five segments.
corbel A projecting stone block or timber support for something above.
crenellate To furnish with battlements; these have openings cut away, known as crenels or embrasures.
crypt Underground room in a church.
curtain wall The wall connecting the towers of a castle, enclosing the courtyard or bailey.
Debatable Land An area of land where the exact Border was in dispute.
donjon Name for a castle keep.
drawbridge A hinged wooden bridge over a moat at the entrance to a castle, raised by chains or ropes.
dripstone Moulded stone projecting from a wall to protect it from water.
dungeon Castle basement or prison.
embrasure The splayed recess of a door or window.
flying buttress Butress in the form of an arch.
fresco A painting executed on wet plaster.
Galilee chapel Chapel at the west end of a church.
gallery Balcony.
garderobe Latrine or privy.
gargoyle Carved water spout projecting from tower.
grille Lattice of metal to protect a doorway or window.
groin One of several sharpe edges formed by the crossing of two vaults.
guilloche An ornamental band with paired ribbons flowing in interlaced curves.
henge Earthwork with surrounding bank and ditch.
hypocaust Roman underfloor heating.
jamb A vertical sidepiece or post of a doorway or window.
keep The main tower of a castle; formerly known as donjon.
lancet Tall slim window with pointed arch.
lychgate A roofed gateway at the entrance to a church for the entrance of a coffin.
machicolations Opening between the corbel and projecting parapet through which missiles could be dropped.
mason's mark Small geometric design in stonework: served to check output and quality.
merlons The uncut part of a battlement.
meutriere An opening in the roof through which an intruder could be attacked; French, meaning 'murder'.

Middle Ages Period between the Roman Empire and the sixteen century.
misericords A hinged choir stall seat.
moss trooper Raider or reiver from the Border region.
motte A steep mound of eleventh and twelfth century castles.
motte and bailey Norman defence system, consisting of earthen mound topped with a wooden tower within a bailey.
mullion Post dividing a window into two or more lights.
mural Relating to a wall; a mural staircase or chamber.
newel staircase Staircase that spirals round a central post or newel.
ogee Double curve, bending first one way and then the other applied to mouldings.
oubliette A windowless dungeon with its only entrance in the roof (from the French oublier; to forget).
partizan A medieval pike.
Perpendicular Style of Gothic Architecture, 1335–*c*.1530.
pilaster A flat flying buttress built partly into a wall.
pipe rolls Important documents kept rolled in the shape of a pipe.
piscina Basin for washing communion vessels.
portcullis An iron gateway at the entrance to a castle, balanced by weights so that it could be raised or lowered at will.
postern A back door; a small gateway in the curtain wall by which secret exits could be made.
quatrefoil A window with four segments.
reiver A raider from the Border area; cutthroat, brigand or cattle-thief.
rustication Masonry with sunken or bevelled joints.
soffit Underside of an arch.
solar Upper living room in a medieval house.
spandrel The triangular space between the head of an arch and its frame.
springing The level at which an arch rises from its support.
squint Aperture in a wall to allow a view of the alter in a church.
Thieves Rodes Well-used tracks that were used by Rievers and smugglers.
tracery Fretted ornamental stonework.
transom A bar dividing a window horizontally.
vault An arched roof or ceiling
rib vaulting: projecting ribs along the groin.
voussoirs Wedge shaped stones forming an arch.